Security

CW01011494

Dedicated to Andie and Lucas for their love and support

Security/Capital

A General Theory of Pacification

George S. Rigakos

EDINBURGH
University Press

Edinburgh University Press is one of the leading university presses in
the UK. We publish academic books and journals in our selected subject
areas across the humanities and social sciences, combining cutting-edge
scholarship with high editorial and production values to produce academic
works of lasting importance. For more information visit our website: www.
edinburghuniversitypress.com

© George S. Rigakos, 2016

Edinburgh University Press Ltd
The Tun – Holyrood Road
12(2f) Jackson's Entry
Edinburgh EH8 8PJ

Typeset in 11/13 Sabon by Servis Filmsetting Ltd, Stockport, Cheshire
and printed and bound in Great Britain by
CPI Group (UK) Ltd, Croydon CR0 4YY

A CIP record for this book is available from the British Library

ISBN 978 1 4744 1366 4 (hardback)
ISBN 978 1 4744 1368 8 (webready PDF)
ISBN 978 1 4744 1367 1 (paperback)
ISBN 978 1 4744 1369 5 (epub)

The right of George S. Rigakos to be identified as the author of this work has
been asserted in accordance with the Copyright, Designs and Patents Act 1988,
and the Copyright and Related Rights Regulations 2003 (SI No. 2498).

Contents

Acknowledgements

I would like to thank those colleagues and friends who have made the writing of this book worthwhile. Their interest in the topic of pacification and their concern with seeking a political solution, indeed an alternative to the current security–industrial complex, has been intellectually sustaining for me. In particular, I'd like to acknowledge the support of those dozens of friends and colleagues associated with the Antisecurity Studies Group and especially Mark Neocleous, Tyler Wall, and Georgios Papanicolaou. Had it also not been for the revolutionary dynamism I experienced in Athens in November 2014 I am quite sure that this book would have dragged on for many more months. Thank-you to Syriza, the Nicos Poulantzas Institute, and the friends and comrades I made during those important days. Finally, I gain strength by being surrounded by some of the world's most inquisitive and energetic graduate students at Carleton University, Ottawa, Ontario, Canada. They make contributions like this book easier to embark upon because, although they would hardly admit it, they make the Department buzz with the excitement of critique and change. Thanks then to Aysegul Ergul, Nick Lamb, Martin Manolov, Gulden Ozcan, Aaron Henry, and Carlo Fanelli among many others, who have made coming to work a joy.

Introduction: Security under Capitalism

Over the last four decades a number of powerful social and economic trends have begun to significantly impact both class politics and how we may theorize it. These socioeconomic trends have been exacerbated even further in the aftermath of the economic crisis of 2008–9, resulting in the re-mobilization of a wide array of popular movements crystallizing with Occupy and Syriza. Bourgeois insecurity has become more acute as evidenced by rising inequality[1] marching in lockstep with climbing public and private policing employment since at least the 1970s.[2] Increased inequality has also coincided with greater rates of exploitation;[3] significant decreases in union membership;[4] and the intensification of the everyday economic insecurity of workers, especially part-time and precarious workers,[5] who have taken on more and more debt[6] in order to maintain a standard of living comparable to previous generations. Emerging into popular consciousness at this time has also been the economic and social insularity of the 1 per cent[7] – an awareness that has produced a renewal of critique aimed at addressing how, in the wake of the Great Recession, there has been no clear political alternative to the retrenchment of neoliberalism through austerity and further global economic uncertainty.[8] This generalized insecurity has taken place alongside the rhetorical rise of the "war on terror" layered over the top of an already existing "war on drugs" and a "war on crime" with their concomitant race, class, and gender implications.[9] War-making as a form of peace-making or "war as peace"[10] has become an essential facilitator for the proliferation of a security–industrial complex inextricably bound up with capital accumulation[11] and Empire.[12] Mass demonstrations against the ceremonial gathering of corporate and state elites during meetings of the World Trade Organization (WTO), the Asia-Pacific Economic Cooperation (APEC) or the Group of Twenty (G20) have cast in stark relief the politics of the 99 per cent with that of the 1 per cent; have drawn visible, geographic boundaries[13] around the permissibility of dissent;[14] and have facilitated the occupation and colonization of urban space for the purpose of "extending the scope of productive labour"[15] and the circuit of capital accumulation.[16] These processes, of course, have a very long history[17] tied to the formation of "police science" and the functional connection between wealth accumulation and the fabrication of a social order.[18] Police science gave rise to a form of prudential thinking and planning that foreshadowed an increasingly elaborate system of risk management and threat assessment.[19] Police science thus comprises the strategic field of bourgeois planning aimed at making populations "productive" through the enforcement of a wage-labor system. It supports, in short, the only war contemporary politics dares not recognize but that has served as the foundation for all projects of pacification: class war.

Marx long ago warned about the embedded nature of "security" with its associated projects of bourgeois social ordering. In *On the Jewish Question* (first published in 1844) he wrote: "security is the supreme concept of bourgeois society. The concept of police."[20] His words are particularly prophetic today in light of how deeply entrenched and entangled US corporate interests are with police power and surveillance.[21] The National Security Agency (NSA) leaks[22] highlighted the reach of Empire and increasingly how tactics aimed at jihadist terrorists have been extended to domestic dissidents.[23] Of course, snooping on both domestic and foreign dissidents is certainly not new[24] but the colonization by risk[25] and security logics of almost all facets of social and political discourse[26] has significant ideological and material consequences. Radical scholars have certainly taken note of these developments but are also the first to point out that none of these trends is inherently new or necessarily a post-9/11 development. They argue instead that "the security apparatus that revved up in the days after the attack had been in the making for decades"[27] and should best be understood as part of the *long duree*[28] of the logic of capitalism through pacification.[29] To that end, analyses of pacification have included considerations of privacy;[30] the response to 'Black Bloc' tactics and anarchist social movements;[31] the relentless surveillance and policing of the poor,[32] precarious migrant workers,[33] and welfare recipients;[34] the infiltration and cooption of aboriginal resistance;[35] the increasing control of protests as a form of insurgency;[36] and even the military mobilization against resistance through air power[37] to name but a few.[38] A prevalent theme that binds these recent analyses[39] is their recurring reference to the materialist basis of pacification[40] and the study of how "productive labor" is imagined and achieved by political economists, police intellectuals, and colonial planners who are, more often than not, one in the same. For example, Neocleous[41] argues that

> we need to grasp security *as* pacification . . . whereas for most people 'pacification' is associated with the actions of colonizing powers, has a close connection to counter-insurgency tactics and is therefore widely understood as the military crushing of resistance, an examination of the theory and practice of pacification reveals a far more 'productive' dimension to the idea. 'Productive' in that what is involved is less the military crushing of resistance and more the fabrication of order, of which the crushing of resistance is but one part.

Elsewhere, I have made a similar point when reviewing the works of eighteenth- and seventeenth-century political economists and police intellectuals Patrick Colquhoun[42] and Sir William Petty.[43] Their works were projects for which "the end purpose . . . was to make subjects more 'productive.'"[44] This involved first eliminating economic alternatives by privatizing communal and titled land and then implementing a system of police to enforce (indeed, inculcate) a wage-labor system. This process was dependent on the use and threat of violence in tandem with a new system of "moral education"[45] for workers – a process that was to be repeated throughout the colonies. Contemporary pacification, therefore, is the ideological iron fist and velvet glove aimed at the continued "forcible expropriation of the people" through a "whole series of thefts, outrages, and popular misery"[46] dating back to before the Enclosures. A Lincolnshire noble wrote candidly: "the lower classes must be kept poor, or they will never be industrious."[47] This, of course, is "why capital constantly seeks to remove all means of subsistence other than the wage" and "why it always searches for ways to force down wages." Pacification is the means by which capital "has to permanently discipline people into and in their role as productive and efficient workers."[48]

Yet, while radical analyses of the waging of class war through pacification consistently point to this bourgeois goal of making workers productive,[49] I think that there has been insufficient attention given to our developing a more fulsome theoretical understanding of the mechanics of this process. To that end, I seek to answer two related questions in this book. First, what exactly *is* productive labor? And how is this realized through pacification? More precisely, what are the constituent parts of pacification that *make* workers productive? Second, what does pacification tell us about the function and longevity of the global capitalist system? Despite radical scholars' theoretical and political elucidation about what an *Anti*-security politics[50] and analysis may offer in opposition to a liberal discourse on security, the very engine that pushes pacification forward, its material foundation, is strangely taken for granted. *I think we need to first understand the utility of Marx's notion of productive versus unproductive labor and, second, examine how productive labor is pursued through pacification.* In the process, I believe both pacification theory and general Marxian political economy will benefit from such an engagement. The argument I will be expanding upon throughout this book may be summarized as follows:

1. We need to understand productive labor as a *process rather than as a category*. This necessitates a critical re-engagement with Marx's original thinking about this construct. I argue that the value of the productive–unproductive dichotomy in Marx's work has been misunderstood and underappreciated often because Marx shifts into different voices with various aims, ultimately muddling the utility of this economic construct for critical readers. If, on the other hand, it is understood

as a gradation rather than a taxonomy and as part of a process of pacification, his notion of productive labor is remarkably illuminating about the intrinsic tendencies of capitalism.

2. We must also come to appreciate that this process of fabricating productive labor is inherently tied to the use of violence and coercion and that these mechanisms of everyday violence are at the core of pacification. The materialist basis for creating "productive labor" is the overdetermining logic of bourgeois (in)security.

3. We can extend the Marxian notion that security "is the supreme concept of bourgeois society" to a materialist grounding rooted in making labor productive through projects of pacification. We can, in effect, say that *pacification is the process by which labor is made productive.*

4. Pacification (as I explain in Chapters 2, 3, and 4) manifests itself in three overlapping strata: (1) dispossession, (2) exploitation, and (3) commodification.

5. As production is more alienating and mysterious, commodities become social hieroglyphs that signal insecurity. These commodities (in general) and security commodities (specifically) interpenetrate one another, imbuing all commodity exchange with security meanings. The mass proliferation of commodities results in the mass proliferation of security considerations communicated at each moment of exchange. Each upgrade signals insecurity that reestablishes the demand for security cyclically. The ubiquity and reach of security thus becomes hegemonic as it is broadcast through both the circuits of commodity production and consumption becoming essential to the maintenance of political, legal, and economic structures.

6. Security technology has become so ubiquitous and has penetrated so widely into all facets of human exchange – from the supra-national mobilization of security forces to the individual choice between competing security-infused commodities – that it is now an embedded and productive aspect of the entire system. The defining characteristic of capitalism, therefore, is its ability to productively sell insecurity to those it makes insecure – in effect, to sell the poison of pacification as cure. By successfully doing so it staves off its own extinction in a

manner that no other mode of production has ever been able to accomplish.

This book begins, however, with a focus on the gap between a general lack of appreciation and understanding of Marx's notion of productive labor on the one hand and the burgeoning scholarly and popular focus on the rise of security and surveillance on the other. I am, in effect, saying that to fully understand one is to fully understand the other: *to understand pacification is to understand how capitalism itself is produced and reproduced.*

Notes

1. Richard D. Wolff, and David Barsamian, *Occupy the Economy: Challenging Capitalism* (San Francisco: City Lights Publishers, 2012).
2. George S. Rigakos, and Aysegul Ergul, "Policing the industrial reserve army: An international study," *Crime, Law and Social Change* 56(4) (2011): 329–71; George S. Rigakos, and Aysegul Ergul, "The pacification of the American working class: A longitudinal study," *Socialist Studies* 9(2) (2013): 167–98.
3. Carl J. Cueno, "Class struggle and the measurement of the rate of surplus value," *Canadian Review of Sociology and Anthropology* 19(3) (1982): 377–425; Michael J. Lynch, W. Byron Groves, and Alan Lizotte, "The rate of surplus value and crime. A theoretical and empirical examination of Marxian economic theory and criminology," *Crime, Law and Social Change* 21(1) (1994): 15–48.
4. Gerald Mayer, "Union membership trends in the United States," (Washington, DC: Congressional Report Series, 2004); Richard Hyman, *Marxism and Sociology of Trade-Unionism* (London: Pluto Press, 1971), Richard Hyman, "The future of unions," *Just Labour* 1 (2002): 7–15.
5. Adrian Smith, "Pacifying the 'armies of offshore labour' in Canada," *Socialist Studies/Études socialistes* 9(2) (2013a): 78–93; Dave Broad, *Hollow Work, Hollow Society: Globalization and the Casual Laour Problem in Canada* (Halifax: Fernwood, 2000).
6. Richard D. Wolff, "The Keynesian revival: A Marxian critique," pp. 103–14 in *Saving Global Capitalism: Interrogating Austerity and Working Class Responses to Crises*, eds Carlo Fanelli, Chris

Hurl, Priscillia Lefebvre, and Gulden Ozcan (Ottawa: Red Quill Books, 2011); Thomas Piketty, *Capital in the Twenty-First Century* (Cambridge, MA: Belknap Press, 2014).

7. Noam Chomsky, *Occupy* (London and New York: Penguin, 2012).

8. Wolff and Barsamian, *Occupy the Economy: Challenging Capitalism.*

9. Jefferey Reiman, *The Rich Get Richer and the Poor Get Prison*, 4th edn (Needham Heights: Allyn and Bacon, 1995); Joanna Gilmore, J. M. Moore, and David Scott (eds), *Critique and Dissent: An Anthology to Mark 40 Years of the European Group for the Study of Deviance and Social Control* (Ottawa: Red Quill Books, 2013).

10. Mark Neocleous, "War as peace, peace as pacification," *Radical Philosophy* 159 (2010): 8–17.

11. Mark Neocleous, *The Fabrication of Social Order: A Critical Theory of Police Power* (London: Pluto Press, 2000); George Rigakos, "'To extend the scope of productive labour': Pacification as a Police Project," pp. 57–83 in *Anti-Security*, eds George Rigakos, and Mark Neocleous (Ottawa: Red Quill Books, 2011).

12. Michael Hardt, and Antonio Negri, *Empire* (Cambridge, MA: Harvard University Press, 2001).

13. Samantha Ponting, and George S. Rigakos, "'To take an accompt of all persons and things going in and out of the citty': Walls as techniques of pacification," pp. 58–106 in *Urban (in)Security: Policing the Neoliberal Crisis*, eds Volker Eick, and Kendra Briken (Ottawa: Red Quill Books, 2014).

14. Luis Fernandez, *Policing Dissent: Social Control and the Anti-Globalization Movement.* (New Brunswick: Rutgers University Press, 2008); Stephen Graham, *Cities under Siege: The New Military Urbanism* (London and New York: Verso, 2010).

15. Rigakos, "'To extend the scope of productive labour': Pacification as a Police Project."

16. David Harvey, *Rebel Cities: From the Right to the City to the Urban Revolution* (London: Verso, 2013); Volker Eick, and Kendra Briken (eds), *Urban (in)Security: Policing the Neoliberal Crisis* (Ottawa: Red Quill Books, 2014).

17. George Rigakos, John L. McMullan, Joshua Johnson, and Gulden Ozcan (eds), *A General Police System: Political Economy and Security in the Age of Enlightenment* (Ottawa: Red Quill Books, 2009).

18. Neocleous, *The Fabrication of Social Order: A Critical Theory of Police Power.*

19. George S. Rigakos, and Richard W. Hadden, "Crime, capitalism and the risk society: Towards the same olde modernity?," *Theoretical Criminology* 5(1) (2001): 61–84.
20. Karl Marx, "On the Jewish question," pp. 26–52 in *The Marx-Engels Reader, 2d.*, ed. Robert C. Tucker (New York: W. W. Norton and Company, 1978), p. 43; Mark Neocleous, *Critique of Security* (Edinburgh: Edinburgh University Press, 2008).
21. Heidi Boghosian, *Spying on Democracy: Government Surveillance, Corporate Power, and Public Resistance* (New York: City Lights).
22 Glenn Greenwald, *No Place to Hide: Edward Snowden, the N.S.A., and the U.S. Surveillance State* (New York: Metropolitan Books, 2014).
23. Jeff Shantz, "On the criminalization of dissent: Deconstructing official oppression in an age of neoliberalism," *ACJS Today* 29(1) (2014): 17–27.
24. Lorne Brown, and Caroline Brown, *An Unauthorized History of the Rcmp (2ed.)* (Toronto: Lewis and Samuel, 1978); Steve Hewitt, *Spying 101: The RCMP's Secret Activities at Canadian Universities, 1917–1997* (Toronto and Buffalo: University of Toronto Press, 2002).
25. Ulrich Beck, *World Risk Society* (Malden: Polity Press, 1999); Richard V. Ericson, and Kevin D. Haggerty, *Policing the Risk Society* (Toronto: University of Toronto Press, 1997); Jonathan Simon, "The emergence of a risk society: Insurance, law, and the state," *Socialist Review* 95 (1987): 61–89.
26. Mark Neocleous, and George S. Rigakos, "Anti-security: A declaration," pp. 15–21 in *Anti-Security* (Ottawa: Red Quill Books, 2011).
27. Ibid., p. 18.
28. Fernand Braudel, *Capitalism and Material Life 1400–1800*, trans George Weidenfeld and Nicolson Ltd (New York: Harper and Row, 1973), p. 18.
29. Martin Manolov, "Anti-security: Q and A interview of George S. Rigakos," *Annual Review of Interdisciplinary Justice Research* 12 (2012): 9–26.
30. Aaron Henry, "The perpetual object of regulation: Privacy as pacification," *Socialist Studies/Études socialistes* 9(2) (2013): 94–110.
31. Heidi Rimke, "Security: Resistance," pp. 191–216 in *Anti-security*, eds Mark Neocleous, and George S. Rigakos (Ottawa: Red Quill Books, 2011); David Graeber, *Direct Action: An Ethnography*

(Oakland: AK Press, 2008), Fernandez, *Policing Dissent: Social Control and the Anti-Globalization Movement.*

32. Gaetan Heroux, "War on the poor: Urban poverty, target policing and social control," pp. 107–34 in *Anti-security*, eds Mark Neocleous, and George S. Rigakos (Ottawa: Red Quill Books, 2011); Jonathan Simon, *Poor Discipline* (Chicago: University of Chicago Press, 1994).

33. Adrian Smith, "Pacifying the 'armies of offshore labour' in Canada," *Socialist Studies/Études socialistes* 9(2) (2013): 78–93.

34. Kiran Mirchandani, and Wendy Chan, *Criminalizing Race, Criminalizing Poverty: Welfare Fraud Enforcement in Canada* (Black Point: Fernwood Pub., 2007).

35. Tia Dafnos, "Pacification and indigenous struggles in Canada," *Socialist Studies/Études socialistes* 9(2) (2013): 57–77.

36. Nicholas Lamb, and George Rigakos, "Pacification through 'intelligence' during the Toronto G20," pp. 213–39 in *Putting the State on Trial: The Policing of Protest during the G20 Summit*, eds Margaret E. Beare, Nathalie Des Rosiers, and Abigail C. Deshman (Vancouver: UBC Press, 2015).

37. Tyler Wall, "Unmanning the police manhunt: Vertical security as pacification," *Socialist Studies/Études socialistes* 9(2) (2013): 32–56; Mark Neocleous, "Air power as police power," *Environment and Planning D: Society and Space* 31 (2013a): 578–93.

38. See: the special issue of *Socialist Studies/Études socialistes* 9(2) (2013).

39. This is not to suggest that radical considerations of how capital accumulation links with colonial practices and the use of force are new. Nor is the idea that central to these processes is the need to make populations productive a new one (see: Vladimir I. Lenin, *Imperialism, the Highest Stage of Capitalism* (Peking: Foreign Languages Press, 1975 [1952]). What is new is the political concentration of these notions into an analytic movement within academia as Anti-security. That is, tackling the security–industrial complex head-on and intervening in the burgeoning area of security studies and risk with a radical focus (see: Manolov, "Anti-security: Q and A interview of George S. Rigakos.")

40. For a useful, albeit abbreviated, treatment of the concept, see: http://en.wikipedia.org/wiki/Pacification_theory For a more fulsome review, consult: Gulden Ozcan, and George S. Rigakos, "Pacification," pp. 1–4 in *The Wiley Blackwell Encycopedia of Globalization*, ed. George Ritzer (Hoboken: Wiley, 2014).

41. Mark Neocleous, "The dream of pacification: Accumulation, class war, and the hunt," *Socialist Studies/Études socialistes* 9(2) (2013): 7–31, p. 7, emphasis in original.

42. Patrick Colquhoun, *Treatise on the Police of the Metropolis, Etc.* (London: Mawman, 1800b [1795]).

43. Sir William Petty, *The Petty Papers: Some Unpublished Writings (Vol. 1)*, ed. Marquis of Lansdowne (London: Constable, 1927a [c. 1690]).

44. Rigakos, "'To extend the scope of productive labour': Pacification as a Police Project," p. 68.

45. Moral education is a theme central to police scientists of the eighteenth and nineteenth century. See: Sir John Fielding, *A Plan for Preventing Robberies within 20 Miles of London* (London: A. Millar, 1775); Patrick Colquhoun, *A Treatise on the Commerce and Police of the River Thames* (London: Joseph Mawman, 1800a); Edwin Chadwick, *The Sanitary Conditions of the Labouring Population* (London: printed by W. Clowes and sons for H. M. Stationery Office, 1842).

46. J. L. Hammond, and Barbara Hammond, *The Village Labourer: 1760–1832* (London: Longmans, Green and Co., 1920), pp. 27–8.

47. Noble cited in Michael Perelman, *Classical Political Economy: Primitive Accumulation and the Social Division of Labor* (Totowa: Rowan and Allenheld, 1983), p. 38.

48. Mark Neocleous, "Unmanning the manhunt: Vertical security, class war, and the hunt," *Socialist Studies/Études socialistes* 9(2) (2013): 7–31, p. 10.

49. In a recent special issue "On pacification," *productive* labour was referred to more than forty times. See the special issue of *Socialist Studies/Études socialistes* 9(2) 2013.

50. Neocleous and Rigakos, "Anti-security: A declaration," pp. 20–1.

1 Productive Labor

In the fall of 1999 I participated in a rally in support of striking public school sanitation workers in Halifax, Nova Scotia, eastern Canada where I was then a member of the local branch of the International Socialists (IS). I held a placard in support of the sanitation staff union local as about eighty of us marched to a local city high school. We listened to firebrand denunciations about the plight of the workers that outlined an alarming story: where there was once salaried and unionized employees of the public sector, the school board had begun to "contract-out" the sanitation of its schools. Former municipal employees who earned a decent income were now either summarily dismissed (with compensation) or were compelled to join the private firm that acquired the sanitation contract. They were paid significantly less, worked longer hours, had fewer breaks, and were scheduled just short of accruing overtime hours. The rally took place at the same time that the "living wage" movement was just beginning to catch on in North America. After the speeches there was even an incursion into the high school led by some IS members who marshaled (they said "radicalized") the students in support of the workers. It was a tactic I had argued strongly against but my protests had fallen on deaf ears. The debacle of dozens of high school students aimlessly streaming out of their classes with only a pretense of interest in the rally was more than enough to push me even further toward my exit from the IS. (It also didn't help that I later denounced my comrades as "paperboy Bolsheviks" before being escorted from a meeting ... never to return.) But in the lead up and again on the day of the rally, I tried to understand why a show of solidarity and such provocation for this particular group of workers was so important to our IS chapter.

I raised this same question with a senior Marxist comrade (who was not an IS member) on the lawn outside the Halifax Citadel National Historical Site. His response was at once familiar and surprising. The white-bearded fellow talked of "pushing back against privatization, stopping de-unionization, building solidarity with the most in need" and, in between sips of his juice box, added, "Besides, they're productive workers now, aren't they?" Productive workers. What did that mean? And, why did it matter? "Well, they are now fully exploited workers under capitalism. They are fresh from the public sector. They are without protection. These are the workers who can best grasp the harshness of the system. They can see it because they live it. They can be radicalized." I already had some idea at the time of the importance of what my friend was alluding to – the notion of productive versus unproductive labor – that at one point played a prominent role in Marxist political formulations. Indeed, in the minds of some Marxist thinkers, it once seemed that everything hinged on this distinction. As if the future of capitalism and the key to socialist strategy lay in deciphering this dichotomy in the works of Marx. I was skeptical, but who could resist knowing what, if anything, productive versus unproductive labor told us about the potential for revolution. Yet, before I delve headlong into an analysis of Marx's writings on productive labor it is important to add some additional context.

Most engagements with the productive–unproductive dichotomy in radical political economy have been colored by the particular political contexts and pressures in which the analysis was written. To a certain extent this is inescapable. But these critiques have often led to distracting and contradictory assertions that have utterly confused the distinction. Thus, contrary to previous analyses I am not particularly concerned here with how Marx's distinction may inform revolutionary thought. I am not at all committed to the notion that by identifying who may be a productive worker my analysis can somehow aid in pinpointing worthy proletarians and swayable managers.[1] I do not believe that there is any imminent need to somehow determine a worker's place on a continuum of exploitation relative to the rate of extraction of surplus value. Or, that my findings may inform national accounting standards in communist countries since we need no longer pretend that such societies actually exist. In fact, I believe that these laudable yet misplaced concerns are what led to our repeatedly asking the wrong questions about Marx's notion of productive labor in the first place. These wayward concerns are best exemplified by the pronouncements of the otherwise illuminating Trotskyist economist, Ernest Mandel,[2] who, in the late 1970s, argued:

A precise definition of productive labour under capitalism is not only of theoretical importance. It also has major implications for social book-keeping (calculation *in value terms* of the national income) and significantly affects our analysis of social classes and the political conclusions we draw from it.

Similar sentiments are expressed by Marxist,[3] anti-Marxist,[4] and liberal scholars,[5] right up to the late 1980s when the notion seems to have become marginal and then all but disappears. This is a rather odd development given that the stakes at one time seemed so high. But like so many other readings and re-readings of Marx (my own included), our times, understandably, seem to dictate how Marx's ideas are re-imagined and re-deployed.[6] My initial point here is that we must replace our approach of looking for precision and finality with that of seeking generality and *process* in Marx's theory of productive labor. We have, in short, been missing the forest for the trees.

While this chapter deals with Marx's notion of productive labor, this cannot be accomplished without reference to Adam Smith's understanding of the same concept. This is because Marx offers a critique of Smith as the basis upon which to set up his own construct in contradistinction. I want to begin, therefore, with two key quotes, one from Smith's *Wealth of Nations* and one from Marx's *Capital*. Both of these two excerpts are widely considered the most definitive representation of each author's core assertions about productive labor. Smith[7] defines productive labor in the following way:

There is one sort of labour which adds to the value of the subject upon which it is bestowed: there is another which has no such effect. The former, as it produces a value, may be called productive; the latter, unproductive labour. Thus the *labour of a manufacturer adds, generally, to the value of the materials which he works upon, that of his own maintenance, and of his master's profit.* The labour of a menial servant, on the contrary, adds to the value of nothing. Though the manufacturer has his wages advanced to him by his master, he, in reality, costs him no expense, the value of those wages being generally restored, together with a profit, in the improved value of the subject upon which his labour is bestowed. But the maintenance of a menial servant never is restored. A man grows rich by employing a multitude of manufacturers: he grows poor by maintaining a multitude of menial servants. The labour of the latter, however, has its value, and deserves its reward as well as that of the former. But the labour of the manufacturer *fixes and realizes itself in some particular subject or vendible commodity*, which lasts for some time at least after that labour is past. It is, as it were, a certain quantity of labour stocked and stored up to be employed, if necessary, upon some other occasion. That subject, or what is the same thing, the price of that subject, can afterwards, if necessary, put into motion a quantity of labour equal to that which had originally produced it. The labour of the menial servant, on the contrary, does not fix or realize itself in any particular subject or vendible commodity. His services generally perish in the very instant of their performance, and seldom leave any trace or value behind them.

And now Marx:[8]

> Since the direct purpose and the *actual product* of capitalist production is *surplus value*, only *such labour* is *productive*, and only such an exerter of labour capacity is a *productive worker*, as directly *produces surplus value*. Hence only such labour is productive as is *consumed* directly in the production process for the purpose of valorising capital.

He emphasizes this point a number of times and in summing up his position at the end of the Appendix to Volume I,[9] Marx[10] reiterates:

> The *productive* (and therefore also its opposite, the *unproductive*) character of *labour* therefore depends on this, that the production of

capital is the production of surplus value, and the labour employed by
capital is labour that produces surplus value.

Before I get into the specifics of my analysis here, I want to make
two general observations concerning the lack of consistency and
the normative implications of both of these definitions. First, I
have introduced both definitions as *core* definitions for the simple
reason that both theorists seem to later contradict themselves by
offering elaborations and examples that thoroughly muddle and
appear to undo their original positions.[11] Second, both Smith and
Marx are not only being "analytic" but also clearly normative
and political. They are speaking in different voices at different
times for different purposes. Smith applauds his capitalists and
their "manufacturers" while attacking the feudal nobility they are
displacing. Marx, in turn, privileges the proletariat and attacks
the bourgeois-thinking Smith for failing to see that wage laborers
are the real source of wealth. Each makes productive those they
seek to elevate and mobilize. Each, as we shall see, takes pleasure
in ridiculing those they define out of productive labor.[12]

Without a doubt, both of these observations need to be attended
to but I want to hold them both in abeyance for a moment in
order to clarify Marx's position as I have quoted it here from the
Appendix to the first volume of *Capital*. It is his anchor definition: one that he always comes back to even after he seems to
contradict himself. Marx disagrees with Smith who holds that any
labor – mental, manual, supervisory, circulatory, and so forth – in
the employ of a capitalist (including the capitalist himself) that
results in the production of a fixed or "vendible commodity" is
productive. While Marx sympathizes with the notion of starting
with the commodity form in order to understand the creation of
wealth in a capitalist economy, he is far more selective about the
type of labor associated with the production process that can be
itself considered productive. For Marx, only that labor that produces surplus value, the source of locomotion for all capitalism,
is productive. "That *worker* is *productive* who performs *productive labour*, and that *labour is productive* which directly creates
surplus value, i.e. *valorises* capital."[13]

On the face of it, therefore, it seems that Marx's definition is both broader and narrower. It is broader in that he seems to be saying that one need not produce a vendible commodity in order for one's labor to be productive. This leaves open the possibility that the worker employed by a capitalist who provides a service to a third party, a client, is productive because a capitalist realizes a surplus from the labor sold as service.

> The same labour can be productive when I buy it as a capitalist, as a producer, in order to create more value, and unproductive when I buy it as a consumer, a sender of revenue, in order to consume its use-value, *no matter whether this use-value perishes with the activity of the labour-power itself or materialises and fixes itself in an object.*[14]

> [T]he cooks and waiters in a public hotel are productive labourers, in so far as their labour is transformed into capital for the proprietor of the hotel. These same persons are unproductive labourers as menial servants, inasmuch as I do not make capital out of their services, but spend revenue on them. In fact, however, these same persons are also for me, the consumer, unproductive labourers *in* the hotel.[15]

But Marx's definition is also narrower than Smith's in that he nonetheless excludes many workers that do not directly or indirectly produce a material commodity, including certain services.[16] Smith would include book-keepers, managers, supervisors, salespersons, financiers, and any other occupation in the employ of a capitalist that directly or indirectly produces a vendible commodity as productive labor. Marx, on the contrary, would want to know whether those workers were directly involved in the manual or mental production of the commodity through wage labor or whether they can be relegated to the realm of circulation. The latter, Marx[17] argues, is unproductive:

> Costs of circulation, which originate in a mere change of form of value, in circulation, ideally considered, do not enter into the value of commodities. The parts of capital extended as such costs are merely deductions from the productively expended capital so far as the capitalist is concerned.

The same applies to rent collectors and bank messengers who, according to Marx, do not "add one iota or tittle to the value of either the rent or the gold pieces carried."[18]

So, while Marx makes room for the possibility that the contract service sector can comprise productive labor, he specifically excludes the sphere of circulation as a productive realm entirely. We may therefore ask: What of contract services in the circulatory sphere under the direction of a capitalist? A plethora of contemporary examples pop to mind, starting especially with marketing firms. So much money is now spent on marketing that some Marxists are considering whether watching television commercials can be construed as a form of labor-time.[19] Thus, even in Marx's most definitive pronouncements, we can already foresee the difficulties of maintaining strict boundaries between productive and unproductive labor. As Marx begins to expand and qualify his definition, the conceptual problems seem to multiply.

As a Category

If we assume a specificity and finality to Marx's ruminations about productive labor then we must conclude that his definition is riddled with inconsistencies. But this is a very large assumption to make. His thoughts were incomplete and the details had not been worked out. While the devil may be in the details the details are also devilishly distracting.

In fact, the details move us away from the more important observation that what Smith identified and privileged as the vendible commodity form under capitalism Marx theorizes fully by revealing the mechanics of value creation upon which it is based. Indeed, becoming embroiled in a taxonomy of productive labor detracts from the element of *movement* and *change* upon which Marx's critique of political economy is founded. Marx is trying to deal with existing *material* conditions while simultaneously attempting to theorize capitalism in an *ideal* form.[20] And, since capitalism in an ideal form exists nowhere, Marx is repeatedly confronted with inconsistencies. We can consider these inconsistencies under three general themes: (1) the service sector, (2) transport and (3) the professions.

We have already noted that Marx maintained that the service sector can be a source of productive labor even though it produces no material commodities. Indeed, his inclusion of such labor is only dependent on whether surplus value is extracted from such service workers in the employ of a capitalist. This rule applies to: clowns and actors,[21] writers,[22] cooks and waiters,[23] schoolteachers,[24] musicians, and prostitutes.[25] But as we have also noted, Marx then proceeds to disqualify the entire sphere of circulation from productive labor, including, for example, bank messengers and rent collectors because they do not add to the rent or coins they handle. But many commercial and residential buildings are now managed by capitalist agencies employing hundreds of workers. And what of bike messengers who carry documents under the employment of a contracting firm? Despite the fact that Marx differentiates himself from Smith on the basis of including labor that is not involved in the production of tangible commodities, he effectively shrinks and confuses his definition of productive labor by excluding labor in the sphere of circulation.

To even further muddle and limit the number of workers included as productive laborers who do not produce a material commodity, Marx then makes the astonishing declaration that the service sector should be left entirely out of account because it is too small to matter and is in any case unproductive:

> On the whole, the kinds of work which are only enjoyed as services, and yet are capable of being exploited directly *in the capitalist way*, even though they cannot be converted into products separable from the workers themselves and therefore existing outside them as independent commodities, only constitute infinitesimal magnitudes in comparison with the mass of products under capitalist production. They should therefore be left out of account entirely, and treated only under wage labour, under the category of wage labour which is not at the same time productive labour.[26]

In his assessment of the service sector economy Marx has started from a rather broad definition in contradistinction and in critique of Smith but has at first incrementally and then in one fell swoop cut the whole sector out of his definition and placed himself back in alignment with Smith.

The second area of inconsistency is in Marx's treatment of the transport industry. Here, Marx makes a special allowance. While he considers the transport of persons unproductive, he defines the transport of commodities as productive.

> [H]ere a material change is effected in the object of labour – a *spatial* change, a change of place. In the case of the transport of people this takes the form only of a *service* rendered to them by the entrepreneur. But the relation between buyer and seller of this *service* has nothing to do with the relation of the productive labourer to capital, any more than has the relation between the buyer and seller of yarn.[27]

But what of drivers operating fleets of buses owned and operated by a capitalist that transport passengers? What if these buses moved laborers or migrant workers? Is not the portability of the labor-power just as much aided by the "the wear and tear of constant capital"? It is for good reason that strange exceptions such as these have prompted some to argue that Marx was making allowances for special labor categories, such as teamsters, because they were an already well organized and potentially militant ally of labor.[28]

The third area of inconsistency appears when Marx makes repeated mention of the transformation of established professions into wage labor. These include doctors, lawyers, teachers, and writers. Marx allows for their inclusion as productive laborers so long as their labor produces surplus value.

> A large number of functions and activities which were surrounded with a halo, regarded as ends in themselves, and done for nothing or paid for in an indirect way (so that professionals, such as physicians and barristers in England, could not or cannot sue for *payment*), are on the one hand converted directly into *wage labour*, however their content or their mode of payment may differ.[29]

The teaching factory is perhaps the best-known example:

> . . . teachers in educational establishments may be mere wage-labourers for the entrepreneur of the establishment; many such educational factories exist in England. Although in relation to the pupils these teachers are not *productive labourers*, they are productive labourers in relation to their employer. He exchanges his capital for their labour-power, and enriches himself through this process. It is the same with enterprises such as theatres, places of entertainment, etc. In such cases the actor's relation to the public is that of an artist, but in relation to his employer he is a *productive labourer*.[30]

If the teacher were a public worker, she would be unproductive. But what if these professionals were "self-employed" as so many still are? Here, Marx makes another grudging allowance:

> The self-employed labourer, for example, is his own wage labourer, and his own means of production confront him in his own mind as capital. As his own capitalist, he employs himself as a wage labourer. Anomalies of this type then offer a favourable field for outpourings of drivel about productive and unproductive labour.[31]

How is this possible? How can someone make surplus value from themselves? Marx cannot be serious. What is the difference between a menial servant and a professional in terms of the content of their contractual relation with a consumer? Why should one be considered productive and the other unproductive? Is it merely that a lawyer has many clients and the servant only one? Here Marx creates yet another category to solve the matter in the special case of independent farmers and handicraftsmen. He says that these workers "belong neither to the category of productive nor unproductive labour" because "their production does not fall under the capitalist mode of production." It is therefore not surprising given this apparent conceptual morass that the most recent tendency among Marxists has been to simply ignore the productive–unproductive labor distinction or, after careful review of the inconsistencies, attempt to exorcise it from Marxist political economy altogether.[32] But are these really inconsistencies?

In almost every instance of apparent inconsistency I have offered in this section Marx either leads or follows up with a proviso explaining, in no uncertain terms, the fluidity of categorizing non-material, non-industrial labor as productive or unproductive labor. My argument is that we have entirely missed the point of Marx's productive and unproductive distinction by repeatedly asking the wrong question. We should not be asking: how can this labor be categorized? But rather: what does capitalism want this labor to be? Indeed, even more precisely, we ought to be asking: how is work *transformed* into productive labor? What are the police mechanisms that fabricate a wage-labor system? Answering the first question, the static question, as we have seen, is frustrating and riddled with conceptual problems. Answering the second, however, is a far more promising endeavor. The answer to the former question, the more common and static question, is riddled with inconsistencies because capitalism *as it is* is riddled with inconsistencies and countervailing tendencies. The answer to the latter question is, on the other hand, far easier to answer. We know that *labor in its ideal bourgeois form wants to create surplus value through material commodity production.* It must be fabricated along these lines in order to facilitate accumulation and this necessitates pacification. It necessitates a system of police science that forcibly transitions all labor into wage labor. It must inculcate a new sensibility about value and work. Indeed, the iconic image of the mass production of commodities suffuses Marx's discussion of productive labor. For example, when Marx creates the odd category of neither productive nor unproductive labor, it is because: "Some of the labour which produces commodities in capitalist production is performed in a manner which belongs to *earlier modes of production,* where the *relation of capital and wage labour* does not yet exist in practice."[33] When he discusses capitalist production in general and first posits the connection between surplus value and productive labor, he does so in the context of the relentless march of the commodity form:

> The more production in general develops into the production of commodities, the more does everyone have to become, and want to become, a *dealer in commodities* a maker of money, whether out of

his product, or his services, if the product only exists in the form of services, owing to the way it is naturally constituted. This *money making* appears as the ultimate purpose of every kind of activity. . . In capitalist production, the production of products as commodities, on the one hand, and the form of labour as *wage labour*, on the other, become absolute.[34]

So, when Marx seemingly dismisses the service sector as "insignificant" to the point of "being left entirely out of account," he does so because it follows that "under capitalism, capitalist commodity production represents the historical limit to which all production tends."[35] When Marx raises the exploitation of artists, writers, and encyclopaedists he wishes to demonstrate that "this sphere [is] for the most part a *transitional form* to *capitalist production*."[36] Finally, in further demonstrating the transformative nature of the compulsion to productive labor he reminds us that "in accordance with the ruling mode of production even those relations which have not yet been subsumed under it in fact are subsumed under it *notionally*."[37]

Outside Marx's direct treatment of productive labor, the theme of *transformation* runs throughout *Capital* in the form of dialectics and historical materialism. If we therefore replace our approach of looking for *precision* and *finality* with that of seeking *process* in Marx's theory then, as we shall see, he actually got it eerily correct. While it appears that he sometimes stumbles, Marx repeatedly returns to the point of his definition – the key to understanding capitalism as a moving entity is through the rendering of labor into a commodity form. Each time Marx becomes frustrated and dismissive when referring to "neither productive nor unproductive" labor, or "notional" productivity, he reveals that the answer must lie in understanding "transitional" forms. We must become alert to the fact while he is never as explicit as we would like him to be, he is building a theory of general tendencies.[38] Indeed, he actually rails against the very traps he then allows himself to fall into. He condemns the "obsession with defining productive and unproductive labour," in particular on the basis of its material content and the "fetishistic notion" of searching for essences through "formal *economic* determinations,"[39] yet Marx himself gets caught up in such determinations when offering examples to illustrate his point. Marx needed to remind himself that when theorizing general tendencies he was not compelled to catalogue all exceptions.

As a Process

By rethinking Marx's notion of productive and unproductive labor from the lens of general tendencies rather than the fixity of the moment, the limits of extant critiques become quite pronounced. In the first instance we re-encounter the normative problem discussed in the first section of this chapter. Marx, like Smith before him, took great delight in capitalism's denigration of those "noble professions" once surrounded by a "halo" to the productive equivalent of "menial clowns or servants." For Marx, this served to emphasize the privileged place of the proletariat in his theory of emancipation but again leaves readers with a confused message because he is using a polemic and political voice. Is Marx merely *describing* productive labor under capitalism as it is or is he *prescribing* a socialist future as it could be through a recognition of the productive role of the proletariat relative to the bourgeoisie? As we have seen, Marx starts from capitalism in its ideal form, explaining that the only form of labor that is productive is labor that produces surplus value. By elsewhere making exceptions and engaging in denigrating attacks from the normative position of a future socialist society he begins to rhetorically conflate *important* or *useful* with *productive*. In so doing, he leaves himself open to a twofold critique. First, that his approach is merely an economic rationalization for a communist politics. His choice of who is and is not productive is based solely on a political expediency tied to revolutionary ends and not a critique of political economy. Second, that whether he is describing capitalism or not, he has erred in excluding other forms of productivity that should well be understood as productive in a socialist future. It is for this reason that feminist critiques of Marx's exclusion of gendered *(re)productive* value have tremendous salience.[40] Marx himself made these critiques plausible when he shifted repeatedly

23

from description to prescription. At the level of materialist analysis, the inherent value of so-called domestic labor is obvious,[41] but in ideological and revolutionary terms the matter is far more contentious because its hidden productivity goes unacknowledged.[42]

If we instead read Marx's assertions as *ideal* and *descriptive* and based on an ongoing process of figuring out the place of different forms of labor under the overdetermining tendency of commodification under capitalism, then these critiques of Marx are no more than reinforcing critiques of capitalism. This can be most clearly evidenced by examining the three areas of debate where the productive–unproductive dichotomy has been played out most prominently by Marxian scholars: (1) establishing a system of socialist national accounting; (2) making distinctions about revolutionary class politics; and (3) predicting economic crises and, by extension, the correct moment for revolution. The three debates are not tangential to our understanding of security. As will become clearer throughout this book, these represent key aspects of the Left's (mis)understanding of the wage-labor system's relationship to pacification. As we can see, these considerations appear to have a potentially significant theoretical and revolutionary impact on Marxian thought but only because the productive–unproductive distinction has been misapprehended conceptually. First, scholars have argued that when they examined the Soviet national accounting system and compared it to bourgeois national accounting systems of the West, there were no discernible differences in value assessment and the measure of productivity. The Soviets, it seems, completely abandoned[43] a Marxian notion of value and were, for the most part, aligned with Smith's notion of productive labor manifested in the form of a vendible commodity. We are now in a better position to appreciate, however, that to critique the national Soviet accounting system as "non-Marxist" is to actually reinforce two points: first, that value creation in a production system under Stalinism was certainly not socialist, and, second, that Marx's description of value creation was as an *ideal* form under capitalism. The fact that Marx's critique of political economy and his labor theory of value are very difficult to represent statistically and the fact that productive labor is almost impossible to disentangle from unproductive labor macroeconomically means only that the existing quantitative and bourgeois forms of determining the value of commodities mirrors the obfuscation of exploitation and the extraction of surplus value under capitalism. Second, to base class politics on Marx's notion of productive labor is to quite expectedly experience a series of inconsistencies and difficulties as Marx himself did when he tried to make determinations about productive labor on a case-by-case basis. Once we move beyond the fluid and the abstract and attempt to taxonomically map the increasing blurriness of productive and unproductive labor, we confront the underlying compulsion of the commodification process as Marx originally described it: to make productive what is currently not productive; to take account of *transitional*, and *notional* forms of productive labor; and to take stock of what is neither productive nor unproductive. So, when Carchedi[44] finds himself slicing in half by half ad infinitum the structure of social classes by occupation on the basis of their "position proximity in the production process to those who perform the function of the collective worker" in order to determine their revolutionary position he is proving empirically through example the impossibility of such a task at its premise. He is chronicling in practice the fluidity and ongoing transformation of such relations. Third, and finally, if one believes that it is possible to clearly distinguish and catalog productive versus unproductive labor at a macroeconomic level, and that productive labor is labor that produces surplus value while unproductive labor does not, then it makes sense to assume that the growth of the relative size of those employed in unproductive labor must signal (1) increasing industrial productivity, the rise in the organic composition of capital (the increased use of machinery) resulting in a relative rise of an industrial reserve army that necessitates (2) the need for a rapid rise in unproductive labor to circulate and consume more and more commodities yielding smaller and smaller profit margins. The rise of both (1) + (2) is thus an indication of impending crisis and the potential for a revolutionary moment. While I am very sympathetic to such approaches,[45] what remains unresolved is: first, how to make defensible determinations about the cataloging of existing occupational categories as either productive or unproductive except as gross generalities that do not belie Marx's original definition; and, second, what precise ratio of productive versus unproductive labor in a world economic system that has witnessed a rapid realignment in the global distribution of manufacturing would be required to indicate impending crisis. While Becker argues that "just as capital compounds interest it compounds the growth of unproductive labour and compounds thereby all the problems of a population that is surplus relative to the requirements of economic production"[46] we have no concrete method of gleaning from either existing economic data or his own model what proportion of unproductive labor would be necessary to break the back of capitalism.

The reason for this apparent lack of application should by now be quite clear to the reader: attempting to catalog, fix, and measure what is notionally blurred, transitional and fluid under capitalism – what will be examined more concretely as the transformation of labor through the pacification process – is distracting and inherently unachievable. Instead, we ought to be theorizing the process by which productive labor in its ideal form is pursued and fabricated: a process we can now recognize as the economic catalyst for pacification.

As Pacification

So far, I have argued that by freeing ourselves from a dichotomous or categorical understanding of Marx's notion of productive versus unproductive labor and by focusing instead on the general tendency of the capitalist system to transform all labor into productive labor we are able to analyse the more fruitful questions of political economy relating to how social order is fabricated through pacification. Indeed, by wedding the notion of productive labor to considerations of security we not only advance theory among those currently engaged with radical understandings of police power but, I would argue, we provide the type of conceptual work necessary to move all critical theory forward in order to capture the enormity of the security–industrial complex that subtends the capitalist system, its historical antecedents, and the logics of its continued domestic and international operations. What this, in effect, means is that to theorize the "making" of productive labor we are theorizing pacification, which itself is the waging of class war rife with resistance and part of a lineage that precedes capitalism. For it is through pacification that imperial elites have always meant to achieve economic and political conquest and control. Under capitalism specifically, however, pacification manifests itself in three non-discrete, non-exhaustive, strata that, at the same time, obey and yet put in motion anew general tendencies of accumulation. Their effects are significant on the social and political realms resulting in a hegemonic and near totalizing presence in everyday transactions. Through a process of pacification, security has come to over-write the ideational and notional via its far-reaching, material ubiquity. These three strata of pacification are: (1) dispossession, (2) exploitation, and (3) commodification.

While different in their strategic targets of intervention, each of these three strata of pacification in their aggregate nonetheless both produce and rely on: (1) the use and/or threat of use of violence; (2) the legal, institutional, and police subversion and suppression of non-capitalist forms of subsistence and exchange; (3) the circulation of a "moral education" aimed at ideologically reinforcing capitalist exchange, the wage-labor system, and bourgeois practices and norms among workers, and, finally (4) establishing an institutional and ideological ethic of security that equates threats to any of these aspects as threats to the state of security and the private property relations it supports. Poulantzas has pointed to similar tendencies in his review of the "state and economy" more generally when he argued that the state's "reproduction" of "the social division of labour" is comprised of "repressive violence, ideological inculcation, disciplinary normalization, the organization of space and time or the creation of consent."[47] Yet, despite his considered attention to the nexus of economy and state Poulantzas, too, fails to prioritize and think through the mechanics of both the processes by which this is achieved through security and the particular ends of this state of security. That is, the overriding objective that will invariably mobilize any and all of these aspects of pacification as I have listed them above is a relentless compulsion to make workers productive through a system of police. The compulsion to create surplus value – that is the core economic condition for capitalism to establish, flourish, and reconstitute itself. It is at once the most banal yet underappreciated theoretical contribution made by Marx.[48] The following three chapters are devoted to unpacking how these three strata of pacification make workers productive – in short, how capitalism itself is made possible and renews itself through these three strata of pacification: dispossession, exploitation, and commodification.

Notes

1. Any attempt to predict with what side supposed bourgeois managerial groups would join during a socialist revolution, I believe, runs contrary to the spirit of the *Manifesto* where Marx and Engels say only that "[i]n times when the class struggle nears the decisive hour ... a small section of the ruling class cuts itself adrift, and joins the revolutionary class, the class that holds the future in its hands ... a portion of the bourgeoisie goes over to the proletariat, and in particular, a portion of the bourgeois ideologists, who have raised themselves to the level of comprehending theoretically the historical movement as a whole." Thus, revolutionary class positions will be based on revolutionary consciousness not pre-revolutionary job descriptions.
2. "Introduction to Capital Vol.1," trans. Fowkes, Ben, pp. 11–79 in Marx, Karl, *Capital, I* (New York: Penguin, 1978); his emphasis.
3. Simon Mohun, "Productive and unproductive labor in the Labor Theory of Value," *Review of Radical Political Economics* 28(4) (1996): 30–54; David Houston, "Productive and unproductive labor: Rest in peace," *Review of Radical Political Economics* 29(1): 131–47; ibid.; ibid.; Ian Gough, "Marx's theory of productuve and unproductive labor," *New Left Review* 76 (Nov–Dec) (1972): 47–72.
4. For example: E. K. Hunt, "The categories of productive and unproductive labor in Marxist economic theory," *Science and Society* 43(3) (1979): 303–25.
5. Kushnirsky and Stull (1989: 91), for example, deliver a concise and well-reasoned overview of Marx's notion of productive labor "from the standpoint of its usefulness in building national income accounts."

6. Indeed, the last time that productive labor received any analytic attention the world was just emerging from the Cold War.

7. *The Wealth of Nations* (New York: Random House, 1937 [1776]), p. 207; my emphasis.

8. Karl Marx, *Capital, I*, trans. Ben Fowkes (New York: Penguin, 1976a [1867]), p. 1,038; his emphasis.

9. The Appendix is titled the "Results of the Immediate Production Process." Marx, *Capital, I*.

10. Marx, *Capital, I*, 1,049; his emphasis.

11. While Smith offers a second, indirect definition that broadly encompasses any labor that creates profit for a capitalist – even labor that produces no material commodity – this definition only appears in an implicit and secondary fashion. This is unlike Smith's "vendible commodity" definition that appears at the beginning of his opus and is clearly and definitively asserted. While Marx makes much of Smith's contradictory statements, later economists have correctly viewed Smith's second, very broad use of "productive labor" as an oversight – that is, Smith failed to mention that he meant profitable labor that is nonetheless used in the creation of a vendible commodity. In any case, the focus of this paper is on a Marxist notion of productive labor.

12. Later, this poses significant problems for Marx as it opens the door to a legitimate critique of his categories based on the perception that they were forged under color of political expediency and normative assertion rather than critical economic analysis.

13. Marx, *Capital, I*, 1,039; his emphasis.

14. Karl Marx, *Theories of Surplus-Value, I*, trans. Jack Cohen (London: Lawrence and Wishart, 1972a), p. 165; his emphasis.

15. Ibid., p. 159; his emphasis.

16. David Leadbeater, "The consistency of Marx's categories of productive and unproductive labour," *History of Political Economy* 17(4) (1985): 591–618, p. 595.

17. *Capital, II*, trans. David Fernbach (New York: Penguin, 1978a), p. 139.

18. Marx, Karl, "Capital, Volume II," p. 134 in *Karl Marx and Friedrich Engels Collected Works*, Vol. 32, ed. Frederik Engels (Moscow: Progress Publishers, 1997).

19. See Sut Jhally, *The Codes of Advertising: Fetishism and the Political Economy of Meaning in the Consumer Society* (New York: Routledge, 1990 [1987]).

20. Robert Albritton, *Economics Transformed: Discovering the Brilliance of Marx* (Ann Arbor: Pluto Press, 2007).

21. Marx, *Theories of Surplus-Value, I*, p. 159.
22. Ibid. p. 158.
23. Ibid. p. 159.
24. Marx, *Capital, I*, p. 1,043.
25. Marx, *Theories of Surplus-Value, I*, p. 166.
26. Marx, *Capital, I*, p. 1,044, emphasis in original.
27. Marx, *Theories of Surplus-Value, I*, p. 412, emphasis in original.
28. Fyodor I. Kushnirsky, and William J. Stull, "Productive and unproductive labour: Smith, Marx, and the Soviets," pp. 82–103 in *Perspectives on the History of Economic Thought*, ed. Donald A. Walker, Selected Papers from the History of Economics Society Conference 1987 (Aldershot: Gower, 1989).
29. Marx, *Capital, I*, pp. 1,041–2; his emphasis.
30. Marx, *Theories of Surplus-Value, I*, 410; his emphasis.
31. Marx, *Capital, I*, p. 1,042.
32. For example: Houston, "Productive and unproductive labor: Rest in peace."
33. Marx, *Capital, I*, p. 1,042; his emphasis.
34. Ibid.; his emphasis, p. 595.
35. Leadbeater, "The consistency of Marx's categories of productive and unproductive labour," p. 159.
36. Marx, *Theories of Surplus-Value, I*, p. 410; my emphasis.
37. Marx, *Capital, I*, p. 1,042; my emphasis. Mandel ("Introduction to Capital Vol. 2.") tries to reconcile these inconsistencies in Marx's writing by suggesting that some labor may be productive for capitalists but not for capitalism – the latter adds to the material stock of commodities while the former does not. I would have less trouble with this interpretation were it not for the fact that Marx himself makes no distinction between what is productive for *capitalism* versus productive for *capitalists* where he discusses productive labor. In addition, Mandel does not insist, as I do, that one general *tendency* of capitalism (that can never be realized) is to do away with these unproductive forms.
38. Kozo Uno, *Principles of Political Economy: Theory of a Purely Capitalist Society*, trans. Thomas T. Sekine (Sussex: Harvester Press, 1977 [1964]).
39. Marx, *Capital, I.*, p. 1,046.
40. Catharine A. MacKinnon, "Marxism, method, and the state: An agenda for theory," *Feminist Theory* spring (1982): 515–44; Angela R. Miles, "Economism and feminism: Hidden in the household. A comment on the domestic labour debate," *Studies in Political*

Economy 11 (1983): 197–209; Linda Nicholson, "Feminism and Marx: Integrating kinship with the economic," *PRAXIS International* (1985): 367–80.

41. Rosa Luxemburg, "Women's suffrage and class struggle," pp. 219–20 in *Selected Political Writings of Rosa Luxemburg*, ed. Dick Howard (New York: Monthly Review Press, 1971).
42. MacKinnon, "Marxism, method, and the state: An agenda for theory."
43. Kushnirsky, and Stull, "Productive and unproductive labour: Smith, Marx, and the Soviets."
44. *On the Economic Identification of Social Classes* (London: Routledge & Kegan Paul, 1977), p. 96.
45. See, for example, Becker's general analysis of the rise of unproductive labour and its connection to crises of capitalism: James F. Becker, *Marxian Political Economy: An Outline* (Cambridge: Cambridge University Press, 1977). .
46. Ibid. p. 235.
47. Nicos Poulantzas, *State, Power, Socialism*, trans. Patrick Camiller (London: Verso, 2014 [1980]), p. 163.
48. And we may add those to whom Marx is indebted, such as Proudhon and Smith – thinkers he chooses to deride yet who first developed a labour theory of value.

2 Dispossession

On a cool October evening in 1970, Alex Ling locked up his Chinese import store in the west-end of Toronto. Pausing with keys in hand, he sighed as he looked up the Bloor Street sidewalk. All around him were sad indicators of the area's steady commercial decline. "For sale" and "for rent" signs hung on boarded-up windows. Small specialty shops, once bustling centres of a vibrant immigrant community, now desperately clung to a trickle of pedestrian traffic. The Polish delis, Ukrainian bakeries, and small clothing boutiques were closing shop. Anchoring either end of the Bloor West Street strip, new subway stations at Runnymede Road and Jane Street replaced the old electric street-car line siphoning thousands of commuters underground. The freshly minted Dufferin Mall was attracting shoppers from kilometers around and the gigantic Yorkdale Shopping Centre and the CF Toronto Eaton Centre were set to do the same. Bloor Street West was dying a slow death and Ling could stand it no longer.

For the next few years Mr Ling and a small cadre of business owners would toil against heavy odds to establish a beach-head in what would become a global struggle for the survival of city centres, village squares, and mini-Main Streets from Toronto to Tirana. Today, Mr Ling is a feted international elder statesman of what should rightly be regarded as one of the most important political movements of the last half-century. While the fight against the rise of massive corporate retail has become almost ubiquitous, in 1970 the Bloor West Village was unique. It was a lone but promising legislative experiment based on a simple solution to a common problem. While business associations had always existed alongside the rise of urban entrepreneurialism, such groups were invariably voluntary and their funding entirely dependent on the good will of their subscribers. Business owners who did not contribute would still unfairly reap the benefits of their more communal neighbours' efforts. The Bloor West Village was the first geographic business area to legally force property owners to pay a property tax surcharge collected by the city, authorized by the province, and managed locally by an elected Board of Directors. Ward One Alderman Boytchuk asked in 1971: "Is it possible that someone went to City Hall asking permission to do something and offer to pay for it on their own?" He answered proudly, "Our businessmen [sic] did . . ." Of course, the only proviso was that after the geographic boundary of the proposed Business Improvement Area (BIA)[1] had been identified, its formation would be contingent on its ratification by 60 per cent of property owners. Once that number had been reached, all property owners would be taxed accordingly. The city would collect the property tax surcharge and hand it back to the BIA Board.

By the time that Mr Ling had approached his BIA Board, however, the BIA concept was already under siege. Forced to pay subscriber fees and seeing no results, a petition was being circulated by disgruntled Bloor-West members calling for the dissolution of the year-old BIA. Indeed, as Ling recalls, the local City Counsellor was asking for the resignation of the beleaguered Board President while the local Member of Provincial Parliament was rethinking the province's role. "Many people were angry," he recalls. "But I tend to work quietly." In 1970, the Business Improvement District (BID) experiment was in danger of being abandoned before it was really tried.

It is a testament to Mr Ling's tenacity and the tenacity of his colleagues that the Bloor-West Village BIA is instead the longest-standing BID in the world. Even though Alex Ling didn't invent the concept, he is widely regarded as the BID's savior.[2] Mr Ling served as the Bloor-West Village's President for twenty-four years, outlasting resistance, doubt, repeated political in-fighting, and even racism to help re-make the Bloor-West into one of Toronto's most desirable and exclusive parcels of real estate. A disarming and affable man, he has a mischievous twinkle in his eye when he says, "I was born in the year of the chicken, so I act like a chicken." Perhaps self-effacing but hardly a chicken. Mr Ling is regarded as a national hero by many of his contemporaries. He has been honored with federal and municipal awards and has even had a community fountain dedicated to him.

While Mr Ling's many adventures in community-building could themselves easily fill a book, my purpose in this section is rather to think through what Ling's local revitalization project turned global phenomenon means within the logic of security. Despite all of its laudable "David versus Goliath" attributes, the BIA movement ought to be understood as part of a long lineage of dispossession central to the development and re-development of capitalism. In 1970, Toronto had only one BIA, today it has eighty-one.[3] BIDs have emerged in almost every major and mid-size North American city. Recent estimates place the total number of BIDs in Canada at more than 350. After being widely adopted across the United States, BIDs have spread to Europe, including to countries such as Albania, Serbia, England, Wales, Scotland, Germany, and Ireland. BIDs are also found in Australia, New Zealand, and South Africa. In 2002, the World Urban Forum estimated that there were 60,000 BIDs in operation across the globe. Using more systematic criteria in 2003, the International BID Project identified 1,200 BIDs or BID-like organizations outside the USA.[4] But the latest statistics from the UK suggests that there are 200 BIDs already in operation in that country alone.[5]

The initiation and proliferation of BIAs are ostensibly about renewal. Yet, they are also very much about security. In fact, almost all of the applications to Toronto's Business Improvement office contain references to "improved security."[6] In many instances this serves as the predominant logic for the implementation of a BIA. In New York City's Times Square they use Community Safety Officers, in Vancouver they use "ambassadors," in Germany they employ workfare security guards, and in Toronto paid-duty police officers. Indeed, the Downtown Yonge Business Improvement Area (DYBIA) in Toronto spends close to a quarter-million dollars on security, advocates for city-centre surveillance, coordinates graffiti removal, and works with the police to deal with squeegee-kids,[7] panhandling, runaway youth, and gang-related activity. It also pays for extra-duty policing while already receiving publicly funded foot patrols from the city.[8] BIAs across the globe have become notorious for their "move along" policies, removing the homeless, the mentally ill, and anyone involved in unsanctioned commercial activity.[9] In Ottawa, the Rideau Street BIA expanded its borders to incorporate an underpass that leads into the commercial district. Why? Because it was largely populated by small-time artists, dealers, and buskers as well as other ne'er-do-wells that put off tourists to Canada's capital region. As soon as the Rideau Street underpass was incorporated within the boundaries of the existing Rideau Street BIA, it was temporarily gated off and then systematically pacified. The Ottawa Panhandler's Union, organized by the Wobblies, mobilized a march to the gates of the underpass, clashed with police, and threw eggs at the BIA's office's. They knew full well that they were being dispossessed of this public-access space. When the Downtown Rideau BIA took control of the underpass, buskers and vendors needed permission from the business association to sell there. Permits were required and the underpass was rebranded with its own website and itinerary of cultural events, including a "weekend artists alley" and musical performances.[10] Since 2014, the underpass became permanently blocked off for "impending construction" that has yet to materialize. The colonization and eventual shut-down of this little tract of urban space, replete with its local class-war politics, may seem like a rather interesting yet parochial event. But Rideau Street, Downtown Yonge, and even Alex Ling's Bloor-West Village should be read within the larger history of urban pacification – a reading that appreciates capitalism's reliance on violence to enforce dispossession. This leads us to rethink the contemporary neoliberal restructuring of our cities as part of a long trajectory of dispossession dating back to the foundations of capitalism.

These foundations of capitalism are based on theft.[11] A theft accomplished via the crudest of methods – the use of force in practice and law with the express purpose of transferring land titles from farmers and peasants to a cadre of new and established landowners. This represents the most primitive yet foundational act of economic rent-seeking behavior.[12] Even some of the most vociferous ideological proponents of the supposed "free market" and laissez-faire capitalism – today manifested as neoliberalism – are forced to concede this robbery as historical fact[13] although many more still choose not to acknowledge this enforced immizeration, adhering to a mythology of some pre-capitalist original position where the best, the cleverest, somehow rose to the top. For example, the founder of the influential Austrian School of Economics wrote that no owner had "the power to compel anyone to take a factory job. They could only hire people who were ready to work for wages offered to them. Low as these wages were, they were nonetheless much more than these paupers could earn in any other field open to them."[14]

This is the ahistorical basis of a persistent capitalist mythology that Marx mocked as "insipid childishness . . . preached to us in the defense of property."[15] Rather, the transition from feudalism to capitalism was the transition of the established feudal classes from that of noble rentiers paid in kind by serfs and renters to that of a new propertied class who, using the power of the emerging bourgeois state, evicted generational landholders and produced new agrarian dependents in a reformed capitalist cash-crop farming system, "freeing up" many more workers who had no other recourse than to sell their labor to manufacturers who could then exploit them in the factories and mills of a burgeoning industrial revolution.[16] A revolution that was financed by established elites who had already profited from generations of feudal usurpations: what Carson describes as "the accumulated loot from centuries of previous robbery by the ruling class."[17] The generational fruits of this robbery meant that the high strata largely maintained their status from 1450 to 1650 such that, as Wallerstein puts it, "the landed aristocracy underwent a process of 'embourgeoisment'."[18] This pattern of dispossession was well captured by Marx in his remarks on the "theft of wood" where he questioned the right of the Rhine Assembly to pass a law prohibiting the taking of wood where such practice had long been customary. Marx knowingly asks the Assembly: "What is the basis of your claim to make the wood thief into a serf?"[19] Of course, the answer was as evident then as it is today: the need to cut off access to communal land and its fruits – to establish everywhere the *right* of private property and its preservation by law and police.

What Marx decried as unjust in the Rhineland forests was, of course, already well underway across most of Europe. The most well-known technique of dispossession was accomplished through the enclosing of the Commons in England.[20] Wealthy gentry would simply claim as private property what was previously largely communal land, open to all for use. The peasantry had traditional rights to the land – rights that were no longer recognized "legal rights" to private property. Traditional rights that still granted access to meager scrapings like "cob nuts . . . brambles, tansy, and other wild herbs"[21] were eventually quashed through legal thuggery: "private property became absolute" so that "all tolerated rights that the peasantry had acquired or preserved . . . were now rejected"[22] – a process that Marx called "the most merciless barbarism."[23] Even if workers wanted to flee to another parish, they were forbidden from doing so unless they received permission from Poor Law Commissioners who would provide for their transfer to manufacturing jobs where they were most needed. Under threat of starvation, flogging, branding, and imprisonment, thousands of former subsistence farmers were reduced to a state of desperation, forcing them into what amounted "in nearly every sense of the term . . . a slave market."[24] A slave market that notably included children.

This pattern was replicated throughout the colonial territories. In Canada, indigenous people were forcibly removed from their land and then starved when they did not relocate to designated reserves.[25] If they resisted, they were executed en masse. Mi'kmaq witer Daniel Paul notes that the execution of the Cree warriors after the 1885 Rebellion took place while "First Nations People abiding around the area, living in various states of starvation and malnutrition, were forced to watch the executions." The intent was clear. As Canada's first Prime Minister put it: "The executions . . . ought to convince the Red Man that the White Man governs."[26] Marx bemusedly cites the English imperialist Edward Gibbon Wakefield's account of the unfortunate Mr Peel who took with him from England to Swan River, West Australia £50,000 along with 300 men, women, and children. Once Mr

Peel arrived, however, he "was left without a servant to make his bed or fetch him water from the river"[27] because, as Marx notes, "[u]nhappy Mr Peel [had] provided for everything except the export of English modes of production to Swan River!" To be sure, this is an illustrative account of the need for pacification – how without dispossession there can be no exploitation. Mr Peel could not compel his servants to work for him because there was insufficient land scarcity and no police apparatus to coerce this labor from them. Australia had yet to be fully pacified.[28] An organized system of legal dispossession had not yet been implemented. Australia, like the North American colonies, at least for a brief time, was open to all white settlers who could work the land.

In his classic *View of the Art of Colonization*, Wakefield laments the cheap availability of land that allowed for widespread self-employment and economic autonomy in the colonies. "The scarcity of labourers for hire", Wakefield writes "is the universal complaint of the colonies", resulting in "exorbitant wages which sometimes harass the capitalist."[29] The solution was twofold: "use of slave and convict labour . . . [or] a preemption of ownership of the land by the colonial regime."[30] This preemptive dispossession was made possible because, according to Wakefield, in the very beginning all land falls under the authority of the colonial government to dispense with as it sees fit. The government could exclude access to virgin land and grant large tracts to land speculators, resource extraction companies, railroad barons, and so forth. According to social historians, preemptive dispossession thus became rampant in the American colonies alongside slavery and indentured servitude. In New York, for example, massive tracts of property numbering in the hundreds of thousands of acres were granted to successive favorites and friends of sitting Governors. In one term, Governor Bellmont is said to have granted three-quarters of all available land to thirty persons. In another case, Governor Fletcher granted to his friend Captain John Evans somewhere from 350 to 600 thousand acres. Similar grants were common in the New England colonies.[31] Each served to preemptively dispossess and price-out new American settlers.

The most vital stratum of pacification, I am arguing here, is precisely this dispossession – this confiscation of lands where non-capitalist land-use necessitates its widespread seizure through force. Where alternative forms of subsistence living persisted, these were extinguished through colonial suppression – using all forms of military and police to engage in class war against non-capitalist economic practices, whether shutting down the entire textile sector in Bengali[32] or shooting at livestock from airplanes patrolling the skies over colonial Iraq.[33] So, where a landed capitalist aristocracy did not exist, one was created to replicate the necessary preconditions for the exploitation of labor. This is a fundamental trait of modern imperial practice and is central to the exercise of pacification. As the eighteenth-century police scientist Patrick Colquhoun put it: "[the] resources of nations are derived from the productive labour of the people" and this labor "is augmented or diminished according to forms of government, and the intelligence, ability and zeal ... in those to whom it is assigned to direct the state of affairs of states and empires."[34]

The practice of dispossession that proved pivotal for the establishment of capitalism in Europe is one in the same for imperial pacification. The "founder of political economy"[35] and the forefather of all modern bourgeois economics, Sir William Petty, makes explicit that in order for the Cromwellian Protectorate to flourish, the Irish would have to be made to work. Sturdy "cottage men" who lived off the land and would only work a few hours a week to augment their income were a complication that needed to be overcome. To make them work and to undermine their subsistence, he recommended that the Crown undertake to dispossess them from their homesteads as quickly as possible so that "free hands" would be available for transport to England where they would toil long hours in appalling conditions. Petty undertook to carve up the Irish countryside into large private estates and then set about forcing the Irish into wage-labor. It is no coincidence that Petty was not only an economic and philosophical architect of capitalism but also a surveyor and imperial planner.[36] He argued that more abundant wealth could be accrued by "freeing" the Irish laborer, creating "spare Hands enough among the King of England's Subjects, to earn two Millions per annum more than they now do; and that there are also Employments, ready, proper, and sufficient, for that purpose."[37] It is no wonder that Marx called him "an audacious genius."[38] He understood long before most the inherent connection between wealth creation and dispossession – more precisely, the connection between land, labor, and the creation of surplus through state power.

For Harvey, state power and accumulation through dispossession are deeply intertwined. He writes:

> [The] state, with its monopoly of violence and definitions of legality, plays a crucial role in both backing and promoting [accumulation by dispossession] and there is considerable evidence, which Marx suggests and Braudel confirms, that the transition to capitalist development was vitally contingent upon the stance of the state.[39]

Where non-capitalist formations persisted, Luxemburg reminds us that pacification's "predominant methods are colonial policy, an international loan system – a policy of spheres of interest – and war. Force, fraud, oppression, looting are openly displayed without any attempt at concealment."[40] The conquest of the land, therefore, ought also to be understood at this point as an act of war. Often this war is open and flagrant and based on clear colonial conquest. At other times it is a war of containment against a domestic populace. But at all times its end goal is designed to make workers productive – to plan and execute a *class* war initially through dispossession.[41]

The politics and practices of enforcing Empire have purportedly changed significantly since the nineteenth century[42] but their inherent reliance on pacification has not. International capital may not be so "primitive" today, yet the logics of dispossession that laid the groundwork for imperial expansion remain central to its function. This contemporary dispossession takes many forms, some based on well-worn tactics of accumulation[43] and some deploying newer techniques aimed at both novel and familiar targets. These include: the rapid rise of BIDs and their related compulsion to colonize urban spaces as bourgeois zones of consumption through security;[44] the importation of "Broken Windows" policing from New York City to Baghdad as a colonial policing project aimed at making Iraq "open for business";[45] the role of gentrification in the re-valorization of urban space conducive to bourgeois land speculation, again accomplished through intensive policing efforts;[46] the similar, but even more violent "taking back" of the favelas through dedicated "Police Pacification Units" in Rio de Janeiro;[47] the "revitalization" of areas of concentrated urban poverty through the intensive use of private security in Toronto,[48] Berlin,[49] and elsewhere[50]; and the criminalization of dissent through the legal redefinition of public space during protests,[51] are all contemporary manifestations of dispossession, yet the logics of pacification that guide these initiatives should by now be recognizable to the reader.

I last met with Alex Ling, the feted Canadian founder of the BIA movement, in the opulently furnished atrium of the historic Chateau Laurier Hotel. Mr Ling was in Ottawa celebrating with family as Dr Victor Ling, Alex's brother, was being honored with an Order of Canada for his research into drug resistance among cancer patients. Towards the end of my discussion with Alex I felt compelled to once again compliment him on his own and his family's accomplishments. Alex smiled, thanked me politely, and sat back studying me as I scrawled on my notepad. I finally lifted my head to continue my questions but Ling stopped me. Pointing at me for dramatic effect, he leaned in with a look of intensity. His pose and lowered brow had a sense of gravity even among the austere black and white Karsh portraits that surrounded us. Ling offered: "This BID thing. It's become a bit of a Frankenstein, hasn't it?" A little embarrassed that he had so quickly sussed out the trajectory of my questions, I could only muster: "Yeah, I think perhaps so."

He nodded his head in agreement: "I think so, too." He continued: "Do you know what I heard at the last international BID conference I attended? These managers were discussing in an open forum how to get rid of their Board Members. There was actually a conversation about this. Can you imagine?" He shook his head in disgust. "They were discussing campaigning for, or how to elect or recruit more cooperative Boards. They were talking about getting rid of their bosses. I couldn't believe it. I was a guest but I had to stand up and say something. I had to say 'Hold on guys, you work for us. We don't work for you. Stay out of the politics.' But, you know, it's way beyond that now. Many of these BIDs are run by management companies in the United States. It's the new trend. They organize the businesses, the businesses don't organize them. They create the BID. It's not grass-roots like it was before. And now they meet and exchange notes and talk about getting rid of their Board of Governors." He shook his head again. "This is a terrible thing."

On a liberal and perhaps "business ethics" level, I do not doubt that Ling's insight about the corporatization of the BID movement has merit. And that, in the eyes of his contemporaries, the romantic defense of the small business owner surely loses its luster when the so-called grass-roots approach is abandoned and reconfigured along the lines of a trans-national corporate agenda. This is Ling's lament. But it is a lament that seems ready-made for any founder of any movement suddenly realizing that the revolution is betrayed. We ought to know, however, that while impressive in its reach and adoption, the BID movement is no revolution at all. It is very much an extension of the logics of dispossession that gave rise to capitalism in the first instance and that fuels its expansion and rejuvenation time and time again.

Through the lens of political economy and pacification, once BIDs were unleashed they could hardly be stopped. Once the Mall and the Mega-store arrived, city-centre and Main street business owners across North America either adapted (if they had the capacity to do so) or watched their commercial strips perish. The only real option was to adapt to the new system of enclosure being championed by the proliferation of the mall as quickly as possible. In other words, to become as much like a mall as quickly as possible. To organize in a manner that placed Main Streets on par with the proliferation of "mass private property"[52] with its associated private property powers over what happens within it. To centralize, sanitize, thematize, and securitize as the mall did. To smooth away the rough edges and to make the commercial strip, not just the individual stores that lined it, a consumption destination. Main Street merchants, however, were at one great disadvantage: the through-ways and traffic zones between their stores were public. Unlike the mall, they could not deny entry, set regulations concerning conduct, alter traffic patterns, beautify or police as they saw fit without the support of the city. They would have to contend with considerations of the "public good," and even concerns by motorists and local residents.

Given what we already now know of dispossession it should come as little surprise that the great political economist Sir William Petty was also keen on city planning and re-drawing the layout of London. We know he advocated for the erection of a wall and the creation of planned chokepoints to measure commerce and track subjects, argued for a national registry and tracking system, and, of course, a method by which to exclude and include the deserving and undeserving. His seventeenth-century plans for all of these urban changes he conveniently called "Emprovements."[53] In the twentieth century, such business improvements would have to navigate a different social and political context. The BID was now up against the mall. Expert managers were required. They devoted themselves to the needs of the BID full-time. They hired political consultants and researchers to assist the BIDs in mounting their cases. BIDs began to organize among themselves, forming municipal, provincial, and even national umbrella organizations. They quickly became part of a well-financed, well-organized lobbying effort that was not surprisingly made possible by legislative reforms enacted by the politicians they relied on and supported to rejuvenate their districts. The BID movement is a rent-seeking movement. It is a legislatively endorsed assertion of private control over public space. It is, in effect, a modern-day dispossession. From the perspective of pacification these developments make perfect sense. At core, they reflect the operational interdependence of public and private order-making and the relentless pressure to extend the logic of "productivity" through the full circuit of capital, right to the site of consumption.

Notes

1. I use the acronyms BIA (for Business Improvement Area) and BID (for Business Improvement District) interchangeably in this book. BIA is the term used in most of Canada. BID is the more widely used term in the English literature, as it has been commonly adopted in the United States. Although, even in the United States, other terms,

such as Special Improvement District (SID), Public Improvement District (PID), Municipal Improvement District (MID), and even Neighbourhood Improvement District (NID) are used.

2. Bloor-West jewelry store owner Neil McLellan, Chairman of the Bloor-Jane-Runnymede Business Men's Association's Parking Committee repeatedly pushed for the BIA idea in the 1960s, eventually resulting in City Bylaw No. 170-70. Many years later, Mr McLellan had a community parkette named in his honor largely due to the relentless lobbying efforts of Mr Ling. Neil McLellan Park runs along the north side of the BIA he founded.

3. Geospatial Competency Centre, "81 Business Improvement Areas," Toronto: Information and Technology Division, City of Toronto. Map available from: <http://www1.toronto.ca/static_files/economic_development_and_culture/docs/BIA_Maps/citywide-map.pdf> (accessed November 2015).

4. L. Hoyt, "The business improvement district: An internationally diffused approach to revitalization" (Washington, DC: International Downtown Association, 2005).

5. As of April 2015. Latham, Sven, "BID Stats," BID Intel. Available online: <https://www.bidintel.co.uk/bid-stats> (accessed November 2015). The site is being continually updated.

6. Chapter 19 of the *Toronto Municipal Code* was substantially changed in 2007, listing additional BIA functions such as "area-initiated streetscaping and capital assets," providing for "graffiti and poster removal services," lobbying on behalf of the BIA and, notably, undertaking "safety and security initiatives within the business improvement area." These were activities that were already being conducted by BIAs in Ontario. The *Code* simply recognized what was already widespread practice. Similarly in the UK, the *London Plan* recognized the need to "support and encourage town centre management, partnerships and strategies including business improvement districts to promote safety, security and environmental quality."

7. In Canada, a "squeegee kid" refers to a subset of youth that use a washcloth and squeegee to clean the windshields of cars stopped in traffic and then solicit money from the driver.

8. George S. Rigakos, "The Downtown Yonge BIA Safety and Security Tracking Study" (Toronto: Downtown Yonge Business Improvement Association, 2012); Volker Eick, "Preventive urban discipline: Rent-a-cops and neoliberal glocalization in Germany," *Social Justice* 33(3) (2006): 1–19.

9. George S. Rigakos, "Beyond public–private: Toward a new typology of policing," pp. 260–319 in *Re-Imagining Policing in Canada*, ed. Dennis Cooley (Toronto: University of Toronto Press, 2005).

10. Downtown Rideau, "The Underpass," <http://www.downtown rideau.com/the-underpass> (accessed November 2015).

11. P. J. Proudhon, *What Is Property? An Enquiry into the Principle of Right and of Government* (New York: H. Fertig, 1966 [1840]).

12. Kevin A. Carson, *Studies in Mutualist Political Economy* (Charleston: booksurge, <http://www.booksurge.com>, 2007).

13. Albert Jay Nock, *Our Enemy, the State* (New York: Arno, 1972); Murray Newton Rothbard, and Leonard P. Liggio, *A New Land, a New People: The American Colonies in the Seventeenth Century, Their Conceived in Liberty V 1* (New Rochelle: Arlington House Publishers, 1975).

14. Ludwig Von Mises, *Human Action: A Treatise on Economics*, 4th rev. edn (Irvington-on-Hudson: Foundation for Economic Education, 1996 [1949]), pp. 619–20.

15. Marx, *Capital, I*, pp. 704–5.

16. E. Thompson, *The Making of the English Working Class* (London: Victor Gollancz, 1963).

17. Carson, *Studies in Mutualist Political Economy*, p. 151.

18. Immanuel Maurice Wallerstein, *The Modern World-System: Capitalist Agriculture and the Origins of the European World-economy in the Sixteenth Century*, Studies in Social Discontinuity (New York: Academic Press, 1976), p. 286.

19. Karl Marx, "Debates on the law of thefts of wood," *Rheinische Zeitung* 298 (Supplement 1 and 2) (1842): 18–32.

20. Michael Perelman, "The secret history of primitive accumulation and classical political economy," *The Commoner* 2 (2001): 1–21, <http://www.commoner.org>, p. 7.

21. Alan Everitt, "Farm labourers," pp. 396–465 in *The Agrarian History of England and Wales*, ed. Joan Thirsk, vol. 4 (1500–1640) (Cambridge: Cambridge University Press, 1967), p. 405 as cited in Perelman, "The secret history of primitive accumulation and classical political economy," p. 7.

22 Michel Foucault, *Discipline and Punish*, trans. A. Sheridan (New York: Vintage Books, 1977), p. 85 as cited in Perelman, "The secret history of primitive accumulation and classical political economy," p. 7.

23. Marx, *Capital, I*, p. 278.

24. Carson, *Studies in Mutualist Political Economy*, p. 133.

25. Howard Adams, *Prison of Grass: Canada from the Native Point of View* (Toronto: New Press, 1975).

26. Daniel N. Paul, "Sir John A. MacDonald," <http://www.danieln paul.com/PrimeMinisterJohnAMacdonald.html> (accessed November 2015). More generally, consult: Daniel N. Paul, *We Were Not the Savages: A Micmac Perspective on the Collision of European and Aboriginal Civilizations* (Halifax: Nimbus, 1993).

27. Edward Gibbon Wakefield, *England and America. A Comparison of the Social and Political State of Both Nations* (New York: Harper & Brothers, 1834), p. 133 as cited in Marx, *Capital, I.*

28. Although the conquest and dispossession of indigenous peoples was already well underway. See: Richard Charles Mills, *The Colonization of Australia (1829–42): The Wakefield Experiment in Empire Building*, Australian Historical Reprints (Sydney: Sydney University Press, 1974).

29. Edward Gibbon Wakefield, *A View of the Art of Colonization, with Present Reference to the British Empire* (London: J. W. Parker, 1849), p. 755.

30. Carson, *Studies in Mutualist Political Economy*, p. 129.

31. James Truslow Adams, *Provincial Society, 1690–1763*, A History of American Life (Westport: Greenwood Press, 1984); Gary B. Nash, *Class and Society in Early America* (Englewood Cliffs: Prentice-Hall, 1970), as cited in Carson, *Studies in Mutualist Political Economy*, p. 130.

32. Noam Chomsky, *World Orders, Old and New* (New York: Columbia University Press, 1994).

33. Neocleous, "Air power as police power."

34. Patrick Colquhoun, *A Treatise on the Wealth, Power, and Resources of the British Empire* (London: Joseph Mawman, 1814), p. 49.

35. Sir William Petty, *The Petty Papers: Some Unpublished Writings (Vol. 2)*, ed. Marquis of Lansdowne (London: Constable, 1927b [c. 1690]); see the Marquis' introduction.

36. Ponting, and Rigakos, "'To take an accompt of all persons and things going in and out of the citty': Walls as techniques of pacification"; Rigakos, "'To extend the scope of productive labour': Pacification as a Police Project."

37. Petty, *The Petty Papers: Some Unpublished Writings (Vol. 1)*, p. iv.

38. Karl Marx, *A Contribution to the Critique of Political Economy* (Chicago: C. H. Kerr, 1904), App. A, fn 2.

39. David Harvey, "The new imperialism: Accumulation by dispossession," pp. 64–87 in *Socialist Register 2004*, eds Leo Panitch and

Colin Leys (Toronto: Fernwood, 2004), p. 74. I ought to note here that my use of the term "dispossession" is more restricted than Harvey's. He seems to intentionally lump processes of primitive accumulation, financial dependency through international credit (usury), and the commodification of labor as dispossession. I agree that these are deeply interdependent processes but I treat them separately. What I have divided into three strata of pacification (dispossession, exploitation, and commodification) Harvey would likely see as part and parcel of "accumulation by dispossession." My goal is to theorize how pacification makes labor productive. Harvey's goal is to theorize how primitive accumulation is redeployed by other means as a "new" imperialism.

40. Rosa Luxemburg, *The Accumulation of Capital* (London: Paul, 1951), p. 452. Although Luxemburg does not identify this process as "pacification" as I have here.

41. Mark Neocleous, *War Power, Police Power* (Edinburgh: Edinburgh University Press, 2014).

42. Leo Panitch, and Sam Gindin, *The Making of Global Capitalism: The Political Economy of American Empire* (London and New York: Verso, 2012); Hardt, and Negri, *Empire*.

43. Harvey provides the following list for accumulation by dispossession: "the commodification and privatization of land and the forceful expulsion of peasant populations; conversion of various forms of property rights – common, collective, state, etc. – into exclusive private property rights; suppression of rights to the commons; commodification of labour power and the suppression of alternative, indigenous, forms of production and consumption; colonial, neocolonial and imperial processes of appropriation of assets, including natural resources; monetization of exchange and taxation, particularly of land; slave trade; and usury, the national debt and ultimately the credit system." See: Harvey, "The new imperialism: Accumulation by dispossession," p. 74.

44. George S. Rigakos, "Business improvement as urban pacification," paper presented at the Critical Legal Studies conference, University of Sussex, Brighton, UK, 5 September 2014.

45. Rigakos, "'To extend the scope of productive labour': Pacification as a Police Project," p. 76.

46. Gaetan Heroux, "War on the poor: Urban poverty,target policing and social control," pp. 107–34 in *Anti-Security*, eds Mark Neocleous and George S. Rigakos (Ottawa: Red Quill Books, 2011).

47. Sebastian Saborio, "The pacification of the favelas: Mega-events,

global competitiveness, and the neutralization of marginality," *Socialist Studies/Études socialistes* 9(2): 130–45.

48. George S. Rigakos, Francis Kwashie, and Stephen Bosanac, "The San Romanoway Community Revitalization Project: Interim report" (Ottawa: National Crime Prevention Centre, 2005).

49. Eick, "Preventive urban discipline: Rent-a-cops and neoliberal glocalization in Germany."

50. Michael Kempa, "Public policing, private security, pacifying populations," pp. 85–106 in *Anti-Security*, eds Mark Neocleous and George S. Rigakos (Ottawa: Red Quill Books, 2011).

51. Fernandez, *Policing Dissent: Social Control and the Antiglobalization Movement* (New Brunswick: Rutgers University Press, 2008); Luis Fernandez, and Christian Scholl, "The criminalization of global protest: The application of counter-insurgency," pp. 275–98 in *Urban (In)security: Policing the Neoliberal Crisis*, eds Volker Eick and Kendra Briken (Ottawa: Red Quill Books, 2014); Lamb, and Rigakos, "Pacification through 'intelligence' during the Toronto G20."

52. Clifford D. Shearing, and Philip C. Stenning, "Private security: Implications for social control," *Social Problems* 30(5) (1983): 498–505.

53. Petty, *The Petty Papers: Some Unpublished Writings (Vol. 1).*

3 Exploitation

In the summer of 1991, I worked at an industrial bakery in west Toronto. It was a dated, three-story brick building that sprawled over three city blocks. I spent eight hours a day, five days a week, standing in a fruit-cake assembly line sprinkling assorted candied fruit atop an endless stream of baking pans. There was flour dust everywhere. We wore hair-nets and masks. The heat emanating from the industrial ovens on a humid night often made work unbearable. Droplets of sweat mixed with airborne flour making tiny balls of dough atop the hairs on my forearms. Our only respite was an occasional breeze of cool night air that would float through a bank of large windows facing south on to Dupont Street. It was a mind-numbing job but it paid enough and I needed to save up for tuition. Over and over, I would pick up a handful of candied fruit and spread them over the top of the dough. I would do this from 3:30pm until 11:30pm. We had two breaks and a twenty minute lunch. It was union policy that we would alternate stations on the line but the foreman ignored the rules. We rarely complained. Some of us were far better and faster at some tasks than others. Sometimes I would be switched to pecans. A portly Croatian woman with a kind face named Majda, however, would always be the smoother. She would hold a piece of four-inch wide Plexiglass, dip it in a bucket of warm water, and run it over the top of the lumpy, raw dough. She would then pass the smooth-ened cake dough in its pan down the line to me. Majda was a full-timer. She was fast but not particularly cheery. She sat on a stool. The rest of us had to stand. The foreman would bring her coffee. He never brought coffee to the rest of us. She took shorter breaks than the fifteen minutes mandated. She even urged the rest of us to hurry up when we took too long getting back to our stations. "Don't be lazy," she'd say and, "We don't get paid to sit." I would have hated her but she reminded me of my mother. The foreman called her the "line captain" but there was no such title. Often, the cake pans would pile along the conveyor rollers at my station as I struggled to keep pace with Majda. I would get grief from the foreman: "What's the matter, George? Can't keep up with an old woman?" he'd shout. I tried everything to slow her down. I would ask her about Croatia. I would talk to her about her daughter, her experiences in the factory, her holiday plans. "OK, George, now less talk, more work!" she'd say. I moved closer to her on the line so there would be less space for her to queue up her finished pans. Crowding her didn't help. In fact, nothing worked. So, I finally gave up.

One summer evening, rather despondent, I stopped off at the shipping bay to sit awhile before taking the bus home. As I hung my legs over the mouth of one of the open garage doors to take in the warm midnight air, I felt a soft thud on my right shoulder. It was a loaf of "Wonder" bread. Our bakery made the iconic sliced bread on behalf of the American company for the Ontario market.

"Braygeesh!" said a happy voice in a heavy Italian accent. "Come on, Braygeesh!" the man repeated, this time shaking the bread bag in a manner that indicated that he wanted me to take it. I reached over my shoulder to accept it. A short, smiling man with wildly overgrown white sideburns sat down next to me and began lighting up a cigarette. He wore the distinctive bright red helmet of the shipping department staff.

"Braygeesh??" I asked puzzled, holding up the bread. I didn't know what he meant. He took a drag of his cigarette.

"Yah! Braygeesh!" he repeated, this time pointing to the side of the bread bag where the loaf seemed a bit dented.

I finally took his meaning and said, "Oh . . . breakage!"

"Yah! Braygeesh!" he replied. "Thanks," I said, and he nodded.

His name was Giuseppe. I came to know later that everyone called him "Joe Senior." I don't think there was a Joe Junior at the plant or perhaps there once was. The Wonder bread was good enough, of course, but Joe Senior showed me over to an entire breakage section. Pallets containing goods dropped or damaged including products such as Twinkies, sliced bread, fruit cake, hamburger, and hot dog buns, and the great Canadian "half moon" snacks were conveniently positioned right next to the employee exit.

"All this time I was unaware of breakage," I thought. Indeed, I had no idea that as my fellow bakery workers punched out every evening many would stop by shipping to pick up some damaged goods on their way home. You should only take one item. "One and go!" Joe Senior would say when he saw employees idling too long along the breakage pallets. That was the general rule among the staff, although allowances were made for many of the women who had large families. Most of the time, staff would take one loaf and one box of treats per week. We all knew that we could always depend on a certain amount of breakage and that this predictable amount was not coincidentally slightly below what would elicit scrutiny from management. Joe Senior was a veteran member of the shipping staff and he would always make sure that there was a sufficient amount of breakage. We were all in on it, but Joe Senior took the greatest risk. Often, I would sit in the shipping bay and watch who would take what. I wanted to figure out which employees were the greediest. Casual and summer employees were reticent to take anything at all. When no one was paying attention and she thought the coast was clear, I twice saw Majda putting loaves of bread in her bag. Most of us never bothered to conceal our take. But I suppose Majda had a reputation to uphold. I never said anything to her about it.

A few months on when university classes started in September I switched off from full-time production to some weekend work. I would also pick up additional shifts on the production line to replace workers who called in sick. But that Fall the mood had turned very grim at the bakery. The prime real-estate upon which the bakery sat was far too valuable. The operation was far too costly. The equipment was far too dated. The union salaries of an aging workforce were far too high. The billionaire family that owned the plant still made a handsome profit from the bakery but they stood to make so much more by shifting production outside the city and selling the land to developers. And so a countdown to closure started. There was widespread uncertainty about the final day, about whether pensions would be honoured, about whether staff would be reassigned to the suburban plant. New rules were put in place. Security cameras were installed. A full-time security guard was posted at the exit. Our bags would be checked going in and out. There was so much security among such widespread insecurity. Without much warning, there was also no longer any breakage . . . even when there was actual breakage. Joe Senior's pallets were positioned at the same place they always were but word spread quickly that we ought not to take anything. I remember how things started to change around the pallets that fall. Quite dramatically, and with very little to lose, the part-timers and casual employees started taking far more bread and treats than they used to. The full-timers seemed to have all but stopped. Such was the mood that Fall. Old habits, however, sometimes die hard.

One day while I was heading for a bathroom break past the shipping bays I heard an awful cry. It was a sad but confused, "Noooo!" Then again, "Nooooo. Itsa Braygeesh! Itsa Braygeesh!" When I turned the corner I saw Joe Senior surrounded by two security guards and a shop manager. It seemed as if he were pleading. The trio towered over him. Marco, an older Maltese man who was shop steward, huffed as he jogged across to see what was happening. The manager, holding out a clip-board quickly gestured to him and then ushered the entire group into the security office and shut the door. Joe Senior appeared distraught. He held his hands up to his ears, dazed, as he walked into the office. It was as if he could not bear to hear what was about to be said next. I really liked Joe Senior and so did the entire bakery. He had a playfulness about him and a twinkle in his eye. It was as if he was letting you in on a secret every time you talked to him. Had Joe Senior's sequestration into the security office not taken place on a Saturday, I believed at the time, management could never have gotten away with it. Whether anything more would indeed have happened was made moot by the fact that there was almost no production going on and the plant was mostly shut down for maintenance and cleaning. Only a skeletal production staff was on site at the far end of the bakery along with about a dozen part-time students shuffling about the plant on the weekend sanitation shift. I tried to linger outside the security office for as long as possible but I had to get back to the line. Another worker who was obsessed with Neil Young had been doing double-duty on nuts and fruit while I was gone and he was relieved to see me return.

At lunch break, I went looking for Joe Senior but he was no longer in shipping. I spotted Marco who was now inspecting pallets and asked him what happened. He had a look of disbelief and anger on his face. "He's gone!" he said. "They fired him," he added, shaking his head.

"What the hell for?" I asked, already guessing the answer.

"Theft!" said Marco in disgust. "Theft," he repeated, gesturing to the cameras that now dotted the shipping department ceiling. "Can you believe? That's it!" he said. "He's gone. No severance. Maybe no pension!" he exclaimed.

"You have to do something!" I demanded. "Do what?!" he responded angrily. "Tell me, do what?!"

I returned to my post and started spreading candied fruit atop the fruit cake dough once more. After awhile the line foreman yelled out, "George!" and then, "Hey, George, what the hell's a matter with you?" The cake pans had really piled up this time and everyone's eyes were now on me. I suppose I was visibly upset.

"Are you OK?" asked Majda.

As the line slowed to a crawl I told them what I had just seen. They listened with great concern.

"They say he's a thief," I concluded. "I guess that means we're all thieves," I added, shaking my head. It seemed like there was a long pause.

"I guess we are . . ." somebody meekly added, this time with an added sense of defeat. A sad silence once again descended over us. It was finally abruptly broken by Majda.

"No!" she roared, seething with anger. "No. They are the thieves!" She looked at each of us intently while pounding her fist on the rollers. I had never seen her like this. I still remember the sticky dough flicking off her knuckles as she pounded her fist while she spoke. "Do you understand?" she pointed at us with her Plexiglass smoother. "*They* are the thieves!"

No one spoke again. She lowered her head and, after a long pause, she said with hushed strength, "Time for break."

The foreman glanced at his watch and started to respond, "But, Majda . . ."

Majda lifted her head and we could all see she had tears in her eyes. "Hmm-hmm," came from the foreman, clearing his throat. "OK, yeah, break-time," he said sympathetically.

It later became known that after twenty years, Giuseppe had been summarily fired for doing what he had been doing every workday since he first started at the plant. We would also later come to understand that he was just the first of a long line of employees to be dismissed "with cause" only days before the formal closure of the factory. They had recorded him "stealing." The temporary cameras and private security guards proved well worth the investment. A longstanding practice had been turned into grounds for dismissal. We were, after all, taking private property. Legally, we were thieves. The security crackdown must have saved the company thousands upon thousands in severance and pension dollars. But the more I thought about it, the more I knew that Majda was absolutely right. They were, in fact, the real thieves. Indeed, the entire capitalist system I later came to understand is premised on this ongoing theft, this exploitation. It is a theft, moreover, that needs to be enforced and then constantly reinforced through the exercise of pacification.

Whereas we can say that dispossession is the act of pacifying through the control of space, exploitation most often concerns pacifying through the control of time – more specifically, pacifying through the control of *labor*-time. Within the logic of Marxian political economy, this is central to the organization of capitalism and can only be secured once a newly dispossessed proletariat is forced to sell their labor-time to survive. At this precise moment, a second, fundamental theft occurs – from the theft of value in property to the theft of value in time. At least initially, it is only through coercion that such pacification is possible – most often exercised by a rising number of "unproductive" managers and guardians of capital within a "general police system."[1] Indeed, as Perelman rhetorically asks: "was there ever a nation where the rich found the poor to be sufficiently industrious?"[2] His answer, of course, is "no." Fighting against "sloth and indulence" among workers seems a central moral theme for capitalists throughout the globe. Although he adds: "no country seems to have gone as far as England in its war on sloth."

A whole series of techniques were developed to intensify labor-time "once capital began to dislodge the traditional moorings of society" in order to "engage people in productive work that would turn a profit for those who employed wage labour."[3] Indeed, once dispossession was well underway, the next stratum of pacification was to establish a system of police for the extraction of more and more surplus-value through the intensification of work and the reduction of payment for labor to an absolute minimum. So absolute, in fact, that a long line of political and moralizing commentators recommended various levels of enslavement. Marx notes that in 1698, the Fletcher of Saltoun argued before the Scottish parliament that in order to remedy the problem of a growing number of beggars a restoration of "the old state of serfdom" was required "to make slaves of all those who are unable to provide for their subsistence."[4] Sir William Petty argued for indentured servitude in the service of debts or fraud.[5] Those who would not submit to wage labor, they argued, would forfeit their freedom. Short of the reintroduction of slavery, every attempt was made to significantly reduce leisure time – that is, any time that the capitalist was unable to accrue surplus. The number of holidays, for example, was successively diminished in the eighteenth century. Up until then, some estimates suggest that one-third of all working days excluding Sundays were spent in leisure, while in lower Bavaria it was two-thirds.[6] The number of holidays in the United Kingdom today has diminished to twenty-eight days; in the United States and Canada the average is ten.[7] The compulsion to regiment and oversee every minute of a worker's day is thus central to the establishment of pacification. This compulsion is based on the capitalist's need to exploit workers in the pursuit of more profits actualized through the implementation of a policing system.

Perhaps the most effective exemplar of this stratum of pacification can be found in the writings of eighteenth-century English police reformer Patrick Colquhoun. It is worth noting that before

Colquhoun was to become famous for advocating a London police that was centralized, salaried, and professional he was a commercial master in the New England colony of Virginia, specializing in shipping and trade. As a loyalist to the Crown he also helped finance a Glasgow Regiment sent to put down the emerging American Revolution. Thus, before Colquhoun penned his famous *A Treatise on the Commerce and Police of the River Thames*[8] and his opus *Treatise on the Police of the Metropolis, etc.*[9] he was compiling one of the most comprehensive statistical overviews of the resources of the British Empire and organizing for the pacification of the colonies.[10] Petty experimented with the Irish, Colquhoun with the Virginians. Both, however, subsequently proposed policing projects *domestically*, aimed at the "indigent poor," the criminal classes, and eventually the entire English working class. Colquhoun's conception of police predictably extended especially to "security [of] Commercial Property" in order for "the comforts of Civil society [to be] eminently enlarged."[11] His "new police" were geared to the benefit of a particular class of property holders, which was consistent with his emphasis on managing the various classes of persons who he said threatened commercial interests. His first police proposals, after all, argued for the establishment of a "pauper police" to separate and put to work those who may fall into indigence.[12]

This class politics was particularly evident in his work for the Thames shippers and London merchants where he set about instituting a system of surveillance that eliminated customary compensation outside official lumping rates (wages). He argued for "the abolition of the perquisite of chips," including "sweepings," "samplings,"[13] and "the abolition of fees and perquisites of every description" in favor of "a liberal increase in salaries."[14] A predictable system of compensation had to be enforced in order to guarantee profits. This meant that pre-capitalist customs such as taking the fruits of what one has worked on with one's hands had to be eliminated as a practice. Colquhoun inculcated wage labor through police at the precise time and place where international capitalism demanded it most – the heart of Imperial England. Pre-capitalist forms of compensation had to be eliminated. Specific lumping rates were arrived at so that "honest labour can be procured for daily wages" and to ensure that lumpers would not resort to what Colquhoun considered "plunder."[15] It was the same type of scrutiny and insistence on workers taking nothing more than their wages that we saw put into practice at the bakery. It was the same logic that saw Joe Senior dismissed. On the River Thames, lumpers were scrutinized carefully, from their precise arrival and departure to their clothing. Indeed, any garments that may be used by stubborn lumpers to conceal customary forms of compensation as payment, such as wide trousers, jemmies, and concealed pockets were banned; lumpers were searched; all ships, contents, and manifests registered and their contents guarded. All, including Master lumpers, were the subject of relentless scrutiny by Colquhoun's private police. Such workplace scrutiny seems unremarkable by contemporary standards. Today, constant inspection is a routine role of private security tasked with shop-floor surveillance. Yet, how alien it must have been to the lumpers who still clung to the feudal ideals of customary payment and the notion that part of whatever you toiled with was at least partially your own. It is no surprise, therefore, that the lumpers sacked and almost burnt to the ground Colquhoun's Thames River police office. There, of course, was nothing close to this reaction at the bakery where, by the late twentieth century, workers have come to accept compensation in the wage form and that anything else, at least legally, constituted theft. We know that Colquhoun persisted despite resistance and that he eventually boasted that his police measures saved the Thames River's commercial interests £122,000 worth of cargo.

Colquhoun's "police machine"[16] was directed specifically at class discipline by uplifting the indigent poor and fabricating the working conditions of the "useful" poor. He believed that "by this . . . a confidence is to be established . . . the improvement of public morals will contribute, in an eminent degree, to the happiness and prosperity of the country." What Colquhoun imagined and then implemented, initially for London's poor dock-workers, and eventually as the model for the entire commonwealth system of policing, followed a logic of exploitation through pacification. As a disciple of Bentham, Colquhoun understood that "poverty . . . is a most necessary and indispensable ingredient in society" in order for a "state of civilization" to exist. He conceded that poverty "is the lot of man. It is the source of wealth, since without poverty, there could be no labour; there could be no riches, no refinement, no comfort, and no benefit to those who may be possessed of wealth."[17] A remarkable admission by contemporary standards but hardly controversial for bourgeois legal and police planners of the late eighteenth century and early nineteenth. Indeed, as Jeremy Bentham makes clear, there seems to be no limit to the potential circumscription of workers' lives.

Bentham, of course, is considered not only a modern architect of the English legal system but, as Foucault[18] points out, an innovator of "political anatomy" for his plan for the Panopticon prison[19] – an all-seeing form of unremitting surveillance where prisoners were made transparent and subject to a self-correcting disciplinary gaze.[20] According to Foucault, "the economic take-off of the West" may have begun with "techniques that made possible the accumulation of capital," but its "political take-off" from all forms of traditional torture and executions of the middle ages was made possible by, what he calls, a "calculated technology of subjection" such that "the accumulation of men and the accumulation of capital – cannot be separated."[21] While Foucault[22] was reticent to allow his analysis of the panopticon prison to stand for a metaphor for contemporary society, Bentham himself had little reservation finding uses for his model. Bentham's list of possible applications for his panopticon is impressive:

> No matter how different, or even opposite the purpose: whether it be that of punishing the incorrigible, guarding the insane, reforming the vicious, confining the suspected, employing the idle, maintaining the helpless, curing the sick, *instructing the willing in any branch of industry*, or *training the rising race in the path of education:* in a word, whether it be applied to the purposes of perpetual prisons in the room of death, or prisons for confinement before trial, or penitentiary-houses, or houses of correction, or work-houses, or manufactories, or mad-houses, or hospitals, or schools.[23]

The interchangeability of housing criminals or laborers is revealing here. In a 1798 companion piece to his Panopticon, Bentham proposes a National Charity Company that would be a privately owned, joint stock company, partially subsidized by the government to have authority over the poor. The plan would start with 250 industry houses but would expand to 500 housing units employing one million workers. He already knew that "human beings were the most powerful instruments of production, and therefore everyone becomes anxious to employ the services of his fellows in multiplying his own comforts."[24] Thus, he was anxious to profit personally from his own schemes: "[s]o many industry-houses, so many cubicles, in which dross of this kind is converted into sterling." He knew the benefits to be gained by controlling every minute of a worker's day. He understood that the profits from inmate labor were contingent on this formation of unrelenting exploitation through pacification:

> What other master is there that can reduce his workmen, if idle, to a situation next to starving, without suffering them to go elsewhere? What other master is there whose men can never get drunk unless he chooses that they should do so? And who, so far from being able to raise their wages by combination, are obliged to take whatever pittance he thinks it most his interest to allow?[25]

Perelman[26] aptly observes that "Bentham was intent on subordinating every facet of human existence to the profit motive." In short, the key theorists and practitioners of the modern legal and police sciences were architects of capitalism itself. Their proposals set in motion a wide array of surveillance and control systems that we continue to develop today. There seems no end to risk identification and risk eradication in a capitalist system[27] because the entire edifice teeters on dispossession and exploitation: insecurity premised on the protection of private property.[28] The compulsion to monitor seems now almost limitless and the idea of complete "telematic" awareness has already arrived.[29] Bentham would surely be impressed by the size of our international security–industrial complex. But given the exploitive intent of his panoptic designs and his clear understanding that workers were "instruments of production," in the service of "multiplying [the Master's] own comforts" he would not be at all surprised by their profitability.[30] The institutional oversight of the sick, mad, deviant[31] and, of course, relentless workplace surveillance has followed the Benthamite logic of exploitation. We ought to see advances in the science of "management,"[32] therefore, as merely an extension of police science itself. The well-documented rise of the intensification and de-skilling of the labor process[33] through, for example, Taylorism[34] is the intellectual and ideological offspring of this longstanding practice of pacification: it attempts to render labor into a commodity form.

Notes

1. George S. Rigakos, John L. McMullan, Joshua Johnson, and Gulden Ozcan (eds), *A General Police System: Political Economy and Security in the Age of Enlightenment* (Ottawa: Red Quill Books, 2009).
2. Michael Perelman, "The secret history of primitive accumulation and classical political economy," *The Commoner* 2 (2001): 1–21, <http://www.commoner.org>.
3. Ibid.
4. Karl Marx, *Capital, I* (New York: Penguin, 1976a), Ch. 27, fn 9.
5. Sir William Petty, *The Petty Papers: Some Unpublished Writings (Vol. 2)* (London: Constable, 1927b).
6. Karl Kautsky, Karl, *The Agrarian Question*, 2 vols (London and Winchester, MA: Zwan Publications, 1988); Joan Thirsk, *The Rural Economy of England: Collected Essays* (London: Hambledon Press, 1984); H. Wilensky, "The uneven distribution of leisure: The impact of economic growth on 'free time'," *Social Problems* 9 (191): 35–56 cited in Perelman, "The secret history of primitive accumulation and classical political economy."
7. "List of statutory minimum employment leave by country," Wikipedia, <http://en.wikipedia.org/wiki/List_of_statutory_minimum_employment_leave_by_country> (accessed 7 January 2015).
8. Patrick Colquhoun, *A Treatise on the Commerce and Police of the River Thames* (London: Joseph Mawman, 1800a).
9. Patrick Colquhoun, *Treatise on the Police of the Metropolis, etc.* London: Mawman (1800b [1795]).
10. Patrick Colquhoun, *A Treatise on the Wealth, Power, and Resources of the British Empire* (London: Joseph Mawman, 1814).

11. Colquhoun, *A Treatise on the Commerce and Police of the River Thames*, p. 28.
12. Colquhoun, *Treatise on the Police of the Metropolis, etc.*
13. Colquhoun, *Treatise on the Police of the Metropolis, etc.*, p. 138.
14. Colquhoun, *Treatise on the Police of the Metropolis, etc.*, p. 355.
15. Colquhoun, *A Treatise on the Commerce and Police of the River Thames*, p. 619.
16. John L. McMullan, "Social surveillance and the rise of the 'police machine'," *Theoretical Criminology* 2(1) (1998): 93–117.
17. Patrick Colquhoun, *Treatise on Indigence* (London: J. Hatchard, 1806), p. 7.
18. Michel Foucault, *Discipline and Punish* (New York: Vintage Books, 1977).
19. Jeremy Bentham, *The Panopticon Writings*, ed. Miran Bozovic (London: Verson, 1995 [1787]).
20. A circular, tower design where the guard or watcher would be central and the cells arranged around him. The prisoner would have no privacy and would be illuminated by a window. The watcher would be situated behind a screen so that the prisoners could never tell when they were being watched. They would have to assume they always were. A process Foucault describes as the inculcation of "self-discipline."
21. Foucault, *Discipline and Punish*, pp. 220–1.
22. Michel Foucault, *Power/Knowledge: Selected Interviews and Other Writings*, ed. Colin Gordon (New York: Pantheon Books, 1980).
23. Bentham, *The Panopticon Writings*, Letter I; my emphasis.
24. "Analysis of the influence of natural religion on the temporal happiness of mankind," pp. 421–50 in *Jeremy Bentham's Economic Writings*, ed. Werner Stark (London: George Allen and Unwin, 1822), p. 430.
25. Jeremy Bentham, "The Hard-Labour Bill," pp. 1–35, Part IV in *The Works of Jeremy Bentham*, ed. John Bowring, vol. III (Edinburgh: William Tait). See also Michael Perelman, *The Invention of Capitalism: Classic Political Economy and the Secret History of Primitive Accumulation* (Durham, NC: Duke University Press, 2000), p. 22.
26. Perelman, "The secret history of primitive accumulation and classical political economy," p. 15.
27. Rigakos, and Hadden. 2001. "Crime, capitalism and the risk society: Towards the same olde modernity?" *Theoretical Criminology* 5(1) (2001): 61–84.

28. Mark Neocleous, *Critique of Security* (Edinburgh: Edinburgh University Press, 2008).

29. William Bogard, *The Simulation of Surveillance: Hypercontrol in Telematic Societies* (Cambridge: Cambridge University Press, 1996).

30. For an examination of this prison–industrial complex see: Christian Parenti, *The Soft Cage. Surveillance in America: From Slave Passes to the War on Terror* (New York: Basic Books, 2003) and N. Christie, *Crime Control as Industry* (London: Routledge, 1993).

31. Michel Foucault, *The Birth of the Clinic* (London: Tavistock, 1973).

32. Frederick Winslow Taylor, *The Principles of Scientific Management* (New York and London: Harper & Brothers, 1911).

33. David F. Noble, *Forces of Production: A Social History of Industrial Automation* (New York: Oxford University Press, 1986).

34. Stephen Wood, *The Degradation of Work?: Skill, Deskilling, and the Labour Process* (London: Hutchinson, 1982); Harry Braverman, *Labor and Monopoly Capital; The Degradation of Work in the Twentieth Century* (New York: Monthly Review Press, 1975).

4 The Security Commodity

I think it useful to end with the commodity as the third stratum of pacification because it is only after understanding its discrete temporal and spatial aspects that we can appreciate how these qualities are embodied within the very fabric of making capitalism. We have established that dispossession and exploitation are essential codeterminant strata in the commodification process that, as I have already argued, may be understood as essential to pacification. We have also established in our review of Marx's notion of productive labor that such labor in its ideal form is labor that produces surplus-value for a capitalist enterprise in the pursuit of making vendible commodities. All other forms of economic activity under capitalist relations are under pressure toward this end. The pacification process leading to commodification continues to place relentless pressure on all business enterprises and fabricates a social and political order that, by extension, also comes under pressure from a set of *compulsions*. Within this third stratum of the pacification process, therefore, there are at least three more component processes that are endemic to pushing commodification forward. We may understand these as compulsions related to the security of the capitalist order. These are the compulsions to (1) valorize, (2) prudentialize, and (3) fetishize. I will examine each of these compulsions in turn before concluding with an examination of their aggregate manifestation in the system as a whole: the hegemonic character of security within an advanced capitalist system.

Before I begin my discussion of the three compulsions of commodification, it is important to understand that commodification does not mean privatization. The latter simply implies the movement of activities that were formerly the responsibility of the state to private interests. This *may* include a process of commodification but not always.[1] Privatization speaks to political reassignment; commodification speaks to economic process. When Canadian public policing organizations such as the Ontario Provincial Police (OPP) try to "sell" their services to police service boards through marketing, wining and dining board members, and submitting competitive bids, this may be said to mimic commodification but it is certainly not privatization because we are still dealing with public agencies. When a not-for-profit security organization such as the Corps. of Commissionaires takes on responsibility for certain aspects of airport security from the Royal Canadian Mounted Police (RCMP) or the local regional police force, this may be described as privatization without commodification. As a not-for-profit organization, the Corps. does not seek to create surplus-value. Thus, there is no commodification because the labor employed to create a product has not been valorized. There is no surplus pocketed by a capitalist. Thus, these two examples simply do not satisfy commodification through valorization.

Ultimately, commodification works through the valorization of labor in the pursuit of vendible commodities. Thus, when the RCMP licenses its image to Disney, Loblaws, and Sesame Street, including an Elmo stuffed toy with Mountie uniform, this certainly is the commodification of the RCMP but it is not privatization.[2] Why? Because in this scenario there are factory workers in China making stuffed Elmo dolls who accrue surplus-value for their capitalist bosses. And, of course, Disney who has contracted them is also realizing surplus at home for their licensing deal (the intellectual labor of contracted legal professionals whose labor is exploited by senior partners) as well as the surplus they realize from the intellectual and creative labor of their marketing and distribution workers. A whole chain of exploitation has been released. Value has been created. And so, the RCMP image has been commodified but the agency, of course, has not been privatized. Let's look at this process more closely.

Valorization

In the summer of 1999 I spent most of my evenings chauffeured around Toronto in the back seat of a black sedan bedecked with security logos. Most of the time I took notes. Other times I went along on foot patrols. My evenings were comprised of long periods of boredom punctuated by isolated incidents of fear. I was conducting research for my dissertation, analyzing the growing private security sector. In particular, however, my field research focused on the rather notorious rise to prominence of a company called Intelligarde. The company called itself "a law enforcement company" and a "parapolice" organization. Both terms would inevitably bring them into conflict with the public police as did their aggressive stance toward trespassers and offenders on the properties they secured. They were, nonetheless, quite popular with many residents and property owners across Toronto and, in particular, with the city's social housing community. Others, however, found their tactics problematic. Posters were put up in downtown Toronto describing them as "Intelligoons" and the Ontario Coalition Against Poverty (OCAP) had targeted the company for protest. Just at that time criminologists, policy makers, and police researchers, especially in Canada, were becoming increasingly interested in the dramatic rise and scope of private security. As a young researcher I had been handed a golden opportunity. Ross McLeod, the charismatic President of Intelligarde, himself a former sociology professor, had granted me unfettered access to his company. McLeod always made the case that his company was a step above its competition. His "parapolice" were better trained than other "warm body" security companies. His company fostered the attitude that situations needed to be dealt with head-on. Intelligarde security officers, therefore, would not just stand by and report to the police but rather "would remediate as required," as McLeod put it. This aggressive company attitude, the numerous allegations of assault, the use of guard dogs, the running turf wars with suburban gangs, and the fact the company had been the target of protests by anti-poverty activists was what initially piqued my interest.

Not long into my field research, however, it was not so much Intelligarde's controversial tactics that held my attention, although these incidents were certainly rich fodder for my ethnographic analysis. Rather, it was something Ross McLeod would often repeat that began to resonate with what I was seeing in the field. "We are a value-added service," McLeod would constantly remind me. I confess I never thought much of this description of his parapolice initially. Even today, it sounds like something any business owner may say: "we are a value-added business." It doesn't mean much at all, in fact, unless you ask the fundamental materialist questions we ought to be asking: "Why do people buy security commodities?" and, "Why this particular commodity?" Up until then, and scarcely since, criminologists and sociologists studying policing, social control, or surveillance rarely bothered asking these questions. Over and over, I would see this "value-added" ideal infused in the very doing and selling of security labor.

Intelligarde security officers didn't just fill out shift reports. They told a story even when there was no story to tell. These shift reports and any corresponding incident reports were written out in narrative form and McLeod's guards were schooled on telling a good story even if nothing happened. They would go into detail about their route about the building, what stairwell they climbed, who they spoke to, even if they picked up some trash, noticed new graffiti, or saw anything remotely suspicious. By the time the report was submitted to the client the entire page ought to be covered in hand writing. Empty lines were frowned upon by the Quality Control Manager who could ask the guard to re-write the report or undergo more training. Report writing was considered a crucial part of being a security guard at Intelligarde. I went through this training for my research and even tried my hand at writing one of these reports. "Think hard," the supervisor would say. "Something happened even if nothing happened." Not surprisingly, I was quite good at writing these reports. After all, I had more than a decade of university schooling on how to produce much ado about nothing. "Clients want to see value for their money," the supervisor reminded us. Our rather uneventful tour of a particular suburban social housing complex one summer afternoon had to be transformed into a worthy consumable for the client. I saw that our ephemeral security labor had to be rendered into a solid material form. In a direct way, by handing in our reports we were signaling to the client: "Here is the security you ordered."

The transformation of security labor into a vendible commodity, however, found its best expression in Intelligarde's then state-of-the art monitoring system called the "Deister" system. These hand-held units were carried by all patrolling guards whether assigned to alarm response, motorized patrol, or fixed at a static site. Checkpoint systems have been part of the security industry for more than a century. In the past, guards were saddled with wind-up clocks with an internally mounted card affixed to the time mechanism. Skeleton keys would be housed or hung in strategic areas around a site and the guard would have to insert each key into his clock and turn it as he made his rounds. Each unique skeleton key would leave its own numbered indentation on the rotating paper disk. This checkpoint system, however, had morphed into something altogether new with the advent of digital technologies. When Intelligarde security guards passed a check-point, they would strike the Deister gun against it and listen for the beep. What was particularly compelling to me about these checkpoints was that they were nothing more than barcode stickers and the Deister gun appeared much like a supermarket check-out reader. As they made their rounds in buildings scattered across Toronto the guards' movements would be recorded on a second-by-second basis. If checkpoints were missed or if patrols were delayed this would be known to management. All of the guards' checkpoints would be recorded and the client would receive, along with the narrative report, a print-out of this digital log of the guard's whereabouts while on patrol. Each checkpoint was coded with descriptors – "21:47:53 SECOND FLOOR FIRE HOUSE CABINET WEST WING" and so forth – in order for the client to understand precisely where the guard went.[3] Here again, I thought, the ephemeral value of security labor was being converted into a vendible commodity. The client received a print-out reporting on the guard's patrol down to the second, a corresponding written report and, if necessary, an incident report.

While it was certainly interesting to witness how the Deister system tracked security employees and how this patrol work was being transmuted into a vendible commodity form, I was even more impressed to see how the Deister system worked when a guard's patrol was interrupted. One evening early into the field research, I attempted to ask a supervisor whom I was accompanying on patrol what he intended to do about information passed on to him moments earlier by a building resident. He shushed me by raising his hand and then reached into his inside pocket to pull out a folio containing pages of laminated barcodes. "Sorry," he apologized, "I need to record this." He flipped to the appropriate barcode and swiped it with the Deister gun. The print-out would later read "22:10:43 SPOKE TO BLG. RESIDENT." Indeed, the guard's folio was full of barcodes for all sorts of common incidents that may delay a patrol ranging from suspicious activity, fire alarms, meeting with police and emergency personnel, and making arrests. This had to be "value-added" par excellence, I thought. Every aspect of the guard's work, as if by the gravity exerted by some unavoidable economic compulsion, had to be rendered into a saleable form upon which Intelligarde could realize a surplus. Here especially, in the service sector that Marx dismissed as unimportant, conducted far away from the client's oversight, with little way of proving that the labor produced anything at all, a way had to be found to valorize the security labor performed.

Valorization, put plainly, means to add value – in our case, surplus-value. Valorization as a constituent component of commodification reflects capitalism's pressure to render all production toward an "ideal" form. We now know what this ideal form looks like: *labor in its ideal bourgeois form wants to create surplus value through material commodity production*. This means that the more a capitalist system matures, the more unfettered it is from countervailing political and social pressures, and the more all labor is pressured to be transmuted into labor in the service of producing vendible commodities at the behest of a capitalist firm. This also means that with the entrenchment of dispossession, labor itself becomes a commodity. How precisely does this process manifest itself?

Starting from the precept that unproductive labor is under constant pressure to become productive, services that once did not create surplus, such as the provision of bookkeeping, security, janitorial services, and so forth are considered a "loss" to a capitalist because, contrary to Smith's assertions, they do not contribute directly to the production of widgets in the factory. Ideally, such services ought to be undertaken in a manner from which a capitalist can accrue surplus. There is pressure, therefore, to "contract out" as many of these "overhead" services as possible. This immediately relieves the individual factory owner of salaries, benefits, training, sick days, holidays, and so forth, but, for the capitalist system writ large, the contracting out of these specialized services further facilitates their pacification through increased exploitation. More specifically, once this labor has moved to a specialized contract firm the capitalist who runs that firm is in a far better position to monitor, discipline, and Taylorize their workers in order to increase labor-time and lower worker compensation. But even here, we have not arrived at productive labor par excellence.

There is still pressure to valorize further. This comes through automation. Wherever possible, labor generally is pressured to automate and mechanize. This applies to all aspects of the labor process and is analyzed by Marx as the "organic composition of labour."[4] The search for competitive advantage among capitalists propels them to rely more and more on machinery with the inevitable consequence of increased output coupled with diminishing returns as competitors rush to adopt the same technology. Far too many widgets are produced, outpacing demand and, unless addressed through a series of "countervailing tendencies,"[5] this stockpile eventually creates a "crisis of overproduction."[6] These are well-understood tenets of Marxist political economy. But as we shall see, valorization presents itself in an especially illuminating way within and through the security commodity.

The structural transformation of policing over the last fifty years has been well documented by researchers and theorists across the globe. In particular, the privatization of policing has been the subject of both substantive empirical analyses[7] as well as the basis for arguing that a new set of theoretical principles is required in order to understand such developments.[8] I will leave aside a critique of this latter assertion to remind readers that the private–public distinction can often be a distraction[9] from the more important process of commodification that plays an integral role in pacification. So, what does the structural valorization of security look like? By about the early 1970s, private security employment (per 100,000 population) in North America had already overtaken public police employment.[10] This is not coincidentally at the same time that workers' real wages permanently stopped growing, household debt climbed, and inequality soared.[11] Today, conservative estimates place the ratio of public to private policing at about 4:1 in the USA[12] and at least 2:1 in Canada.[13] Similar growth has been reported in the UK,[14] Germany,[15] Greece,[16] Poland,[17] the Netherlands,[18] and the rest of Europe.[19] Despite the fact that public expenditures on policing grew consistently in the aftermath of the Organization of the Petroleum Exporting Countries (OPEC) crisis, private security employment continues to rise sharply in most industrialized nations.[20] In the wake of the collapse of the Soviet system, the liberalization of markets in the former Eastern Bloc, and the sudden glut of trained state security agents with strong ties to former communist apparatchiks, Eastern European nations,[21] the Ukraine and Russia[22] all saw sudden booms in private security. In some cases, the state had little choice but to attempt to legalize and regulate what was already fast becoming a system-wide protection racket economy.[23] This also meant widespread licensing and monitoring, the formation of industry associations, and the increased global concentration of contract private security provision. In 2002, for example, the Confederation of European Security Services (CoESS), an umbrella organization for national private security associations in Europe, was established with the objective of "harmonization of national legislation" to foster open competition for security services in all member states. Today CoESS is undergoing another expansion as it assesses the inclusion of new member states and even non-member states from the former Eastern Bloc, Asia, and Africa.

Prior to the formation of CoESS, Group 4 Falck of Denmark merged with G4S of Britain and adopted the latter's name, making it the world's largest security service provider. The company had already announced ten takeovers in Germany by 2001.[24] In 1999, Securitas AB, their only substantial international competitor employing more than 210,000 people worldwide, purchased Pinkerton in the USA, which increased Securitas' employee pool by another 117,000.[25] Not to be outdone, G4S bought Wackenhut in 2002, a leading US security company that operates dozens of private prisons. Today, G4S operates in 110 countries, and employs more than 600,000 security guards from Lesotho to Luxemburg and is the largest security provider in the world. As an exemplar of the ubiquitous nature of contemporary security provision, G4S runs detention facilities in Australia, mining operations in Indonesia, and rock concerts in London. Across the globe, trade liberalization and "contracting out" policies under neo-liberalism have helped the security industry prosper. Security firms are now engaged in policing functions that only decades previously would have been viewed as a public responsibility: patrols of outdoor business districts and massive urban commercial and residential complexes and the guarding of penal institutions, nuclear facilities, seaports, airports, and even police stations.[26]

Not surprisingly, these developments follow precisely the compulsion to valorize security labor. The industry has moved from in-house to contract security for hire[27] to closed-circuit television (CCTV), and on to security software and other automated systems.[28] While there is a clear movement from less to more valorized forms of security provision no form is ever entirely superseded by another. Services previously provided by the public police or in-house security employees have been contracted out to larger and larger multinational security agencies, centralizing both capital accumulation and control over security workers. This has ensured that as security labor plays a pivotal role in the pacification of other labor generally, security labor itself is more insecure by virtue of its increased automation and precarity. Each technological innovation seeks to automate security labor in order to eventually replace it. For years, security guards have been increasingly fitted with monitoring equipment linked to Global Positioning and centralized dispatch systems. The reams of information that they collect are then sold back to the client as proof of the "productivity" of the security staff the client has contracted.[29]

The manufacturing of such equipment is clearly productive. The attempt to render the ephemeral and fleeting character of security labor as a vendible commodity here is largely representational but the pull of valorization cannot be ignored. Electronic checkpoints are visited and the client can often check this in real time. Even the reporting of occurrences and interactions with the public are reimagined through report codes. This is the case of the Intelligarde security guards who, as we have seen, carry notebooks full of laminated pages of barcodes representing corresponding incidents that they must scan when something arises.[30] It is important to appreciate that the incident represents a commercial transaction as the security guard swipes a corresponding barcode that most appropriately matches the interaction: from "spoke to residents" to "arrest for trespass" to "assisted police." The security firm knows the average time it takes to clear each incident because their guards are routinely providing data for analysis. When incidents take longer than they should, a Quality Control Manager can make further inquiries. Each minute of a security guard's shift is accounted for. There is an attempt through this automation and auto-surveillance to make the guard into a producer of a vendible commodity. Clients get a print-out (or digital report) of the whereabouts of the security personnel and the incidents they were involved in.[31] What makes the commodification of security special is precisely this process by which it is both a vehicle for valorizing labor while it is itself increasingly valorized.

Last year, the first purported robot security guard made its appearance in California's Silicon Valley. Touted as a cross between R2-D2 and WALL·E's girlfriend[32] the K5 Knightscope can be leased for $6.25 an hour, which is "about half the price of the average security guard." There are, of course, many advantages to robot over human patrol. "They'll work triple shift, 24 hours a day. The battery is supposed to last around a day and when it runs out they go back to a charging carpet and in 20 minutes they are charged up again." But, more importantly, the manufacturer of this newest security commodity employs dozens of factory workers from whom a capitalist accrues direct surplus. The fabrication and assembly of all of the components necessary for the K5 and its myriad sensors[33] is the end goal of the valorization of security. Along the way the K5 is monitoring its patrol route as an "autonomous data machine," constantly recording and adding more value by collecting streams of video and sensory information far in excess of a live guard. Of course, this is not to suggest that all security labor is destined to be roboticized. This is not my point. Rather, this is merely to illustrate that the natural proclivity of capitalism is to valorize all human activity in this manner. It has been as true for the auto sector as it has been for food packaging.[34] So, the particular development of the security commodity in this manner certainly can also be found elsewhere in the production and consumption cycle of capitalism. It is not endemic to security. George Lucas' Star Wars franchise is probably the most famous example. From film to conventions to lunch boxes and T-shirts to almost any manner of commodity under license. The process by which the initial performance is transformed through to its valorization, recirculation as various DVD incarnations, and representation as a vendible commodity for exchange is merely an answer to a prime locomotive force in the creation of value. All along the way, armies of workers have been dispatched to make value out of thin air. To accrue surplus. There are thousands of similar examples.

What makes the security commodity special is that it is both the valorizing force that makes this surplus-value possible while simultaneously being subject to the very same process of commodification. So, despite the fact that valorization is part of a generalized process of commodification under capitalism the security commodity is especially crucial. We see today that the oversight of labor is itself accomplished through manifestations of valorized security labor everywhere. These vendible security commodities, whether in the form of mundane CCTV monitoring or even future robot guards, are material manifestations of what Marx calls "dead labour." These security commodities intensify production through ongoing surveillance while themselves reflecting this very same valorization. They can facilitate the recording of almost every aspect of shop floor activity, thereby providing all the necessary data to manage a wide array of risks through prudential thinking.

Prudentialization

Soon after I became Chair of my Department in 2011 I was confronted with an unexpected dilemma. Our unit had recently turned over the everyday staffing, booking, and use of our resource centre to our undergraduate student association. This was a positive initiative because it allowed students access to the space for after-hours study, alleviated the Department's burden of staffing, and created an opportunity for students to run their own affairs while building volunteer experience by managing the space. We even wrote letters of reference for students who took on this extra responsibility. The students built a website for the resource library complete with online booking and even raised monies to better furnish the room. Everything was fine until two issues emerged that made all of this problematic. First, there was a recently well-publicized after-hours incident of sexual assault on campus around the time we opened up the resource centre for wider use. A female student working in an isolated lab on campus had been attacked and the assailant was still at large. Second, a senior member of my Department reminded me that there were some relatively valuable books that had been donated to the resource centre. In the absence of a librarian or manager who could safeguard the books and lock the doors after 5:00pm coupled with the increased after-hours use of the space by students, we were inviting theft. The opening up of the library, it seemed, had resulted in unforeseen risks to property and persons. When I consulted with campus security, the solution seemed obvious: if we paid for the initial installation costs campus security could monitor and record activities in the resource room via a new high-definition CCTV camera.

Now, given my previous critical work on social control and policing I was not keen to oversee the installation of a surveillance camera in my Department. Even though I could rationalize its use I knew that, in the end, I would look hypocritical. More than this, I would have to use Department funds. So, I reluctantly brought this matter before the Department Board. Eventually, and with some degree of consternation and only with the support of the undergraduate society, the camera was installed along with a sign indicating that the room was under surveillance. The students requested this notice in order to achieve informed consent and as a general deterrent. Some time after the affair was settled a junior faculty member visited my office to discuss the matter further. She began by expressing her discomfort with the installation of the camera. I agreed. But when weighing all the risks she finally shrugged: "I guess it's the prudent thing to do." Once again I agreed but it certainly occurred to both of us at the time just how easily institutional risk management comes to dominate decision-making. As Head of my Department I was, of course, also a risk manager. I had to be prudent.

Prudentialization refers to the process by which all commodity production in a capitalist economy is increasingly imbued with security planning and risk calculation within its circuits of production and consumption. Security becomes a fundamental characteristic for the making of goods. The operational logic through which this prudentialization is most clearly mobilized and recognizable today is "risk management." To be sure, risk and prudential thought have a very long history. They are part of the development of the scientific method that took place alongside the evolution of mathematics during the Enlightenment. Risk calculation met the demands of an emerging merchant class that needed to hedge against the costs of their entrepreneurial ventures. Hadden[35] has argued that the development of mathematics, and I would suggest by extension risk calculation, is in fact indebted to merchant accounting above all else. Innovations in and the proliferation of mathematics, initially throughout the East and through the Mediterranean, are based on the needs of commercial interests.

Prudentialism is based on a probability calculation but it is not a value-neutral determination. Risk, as it has come to be understood by the institutions that make up the capitalist structure, ought to be thought as harms against goods.[36] That is, risks against profitability and the viability of value creation. So, while history is replete with ancient games of chance, hand-carved dice that are remarkably randomized,[37] or all forms of betting ledgers that used rudimentary mathematics to infer probabilities,[38] risk does not really become risk as we know it until it is developed as "risico at sea" initially by the Genovese and then eventually as schemes developed by bourgeois thinkers around Lloyd's coffee house in seventeenth-century London. According to Cockerell and Green[39] marine policies begin in thirteenth-century Palermo and Genoa and were likely introduced to London in the fifteenth century. Marine insurance premiums were set on the basis of the size and qualities of ships and cargoes as well as evaluations of routes and destinations. These are the precursors of rationale risk assessment that comes to fruition in the seventeenth century. Such "contingency planning" had broad financial aims requiring the collection and analysis of statistical data. There was ongoing evaluation of rational or "structural" risks as well as natural disasters. Actuarial science was being put to use for "the protection or *policing of capital* investment and traded commodities by 'technical' or 'financial' means."[40] Lightning conductors, for example, were an established form of technical risk management by the eighteenth century, while insurance schemes were also being advanced. Even Petty, in association with Samuel Hartlib, advocated for agricultural insurance as early as the late seventeenth century – a scheme, of course, from which they would both benefit handsomely. So, while there is early evidence of ancient types of insurance in the form of protection tributes and shared losses among seagoing flotillas that date back to the Babylonians, Persians, Athenians, and Romans, the development of the modern-day insurance contract did not appear until the fourteenth century[41] and then, as before, as a method to offsets risks associated with international commerce.

The widespread dissemination of risk knowledge was fostered by the insurance industry and the type of statistical and actuarial calculations that became increasingly accessible after the Second World War. In cooperation with their German subsidiary, Hollerith IBM was instrumental in developing collation and eventually correlational computational machines (initially as card sorters) during the war. Hollerith machine technologies were first developed specifically to sift through mountains of birth, death, and marriage census data to identify Jews for transport to concentration camps.[42] As Nazi troops marched into newly conquered

Polish and Czech towns they came with lists of identified Jews for transport to the concentration camps. It was in keeping with the logic of Bentham's panoptic designs and a clear precursor to modern dataveillance.[43] This computational breakthrough was specifically developed to commit genocide. It was *panopticide*. It ought to come as little surprise by now that the development of a technology necessary for the identification of suitable enemies[44] of the state made its most significant breakthrough as an instrument of war and pacification. Like other sectors of the military–industrial complex, Nazi science was harnessed by the United States for its own advantage. It was not only the rocketeers and physicists[45] who made a substantial impact on the American state but so did returning military personnel who set about implementing logistical and planning practices that were to become central to corporate strategy and eventually helped set the stage for postwar America's capitalist hegemony. Indeed, one may argue that this frenzy of mathematical cleverness, the vying for whatever edge may present itself in identifying value, has become more pronounced than ever, shaping everything from baseball[46] to high-speed trading.[47] The corporate and institutional halls of Empire now hum to the motor of risk calculation.

This proliferation of risk thinking has not gone unnoticed by social scientists. Ulrich Beck[48] has argued that contemporary society is now a world "risk society" as unremitting risk from nuclear annihilation and ecological catastrophe threaten the very survival of humanity. So strong is this sense of risk that Beck has argued that no one can escape it. That "smog is democratic" and that risk consciousness has replaced class consciousness as a characteristic of modern life. Even as science seeks answers to known risks today, it produces more unknown risks into the future. This has the persistent effect of setting up a general sense of unease and distrust with risk experts. Yet the more risk sensitive we become, the more we nonetheless turn to risk experts and their solutions for help. He calls this "a system immanent normal form of the revolutionizing of needs" or a "boomerang effect" where every solution produces a new series of long-term unforeseen risks. This ontological insecurity has been expressed elsewhere as a condition of modernity by Giddens.[49] That is, our awareness of risk has become so pervasive that it colors our interactions with institutions, individuals, and even our everyday urban surroundings.[50] There is strong empirical evidence that we have indeed internalized risk. The roaming distances of our children have progressively shrunk, and we have seen new terms such as "play dates" and "helicopter parents" enter our vocabulary.[51] But more than this, there is a general sense of powerlessness about the inevitability of school shootings, terrorist attacks, and child abductions no matter how statistically unlikely – no doubt amplified by the connectedness and immediacy of news[52] and its twenty-four hour cycle.

It is no surprise, therefore, that the lead institution in the framing and response to risk are the police. They act as the hub for the coordination of security mobilizations[53] in both public and private settings. The public police collaborate with insurance companies to reduce drunk driving through roadside sobriety checkpoints and they produce a wealth of accident data for insurance actuaries.[54] Indeed, the police also engage in community risk reduction strategies such as home security audits, financed directly by the insurance industry.[55] Homeowners are advised of the security threats in their home and offered contacts and services to help make their homes more burglar-proof. This "target hardening" is considered a public good because overall opportunity crime is reduced. Of course, if homeowners do not take steps to remedy these security deficiencies then they could be denied future claims or dropped from the policy altogether. The public–private distinction here becomes increasingly irrelevant from the perspective of political economy. What matters is not a "civics class" consideration of whether the public police ought to be using their authority to aid the insurance industry in their inspections of homes. After all, the insurance industry could be far more coercive by deploying its own inspectorate if it wanted to, linking policy renewal to home inspection. This is not what matters most for understanding the commodification of security. What matters most is how the homeowner and his or her home have become prudentialized – coded through the knowledge of riskiness. Both are conditioned through a "risk market," which is "characterized [by] the selling of commodified social control" through "fear" and the "continued consumerization of citizens."[56] The solution comes in the form of more security commodities, ranging from stronger doors, to home alarms to iron bars and even home-based CCTV. Examples of the ubiquity of risk are manifold and can be found throughout the entire circuit of production to consumption and are embedded within the wider political and social context. The point here is that risk management finds both its problematization and the impossibility of its long-term satiation within the commodity. Risk springs forth from the commodity while at the same time spawning its risk-management solution, yet again manifested as a security commodity, and yet again prone to more unanticipated risks. The communicator for this relentless and ever-expanding nexus of risk is therefore the commodity. This dialectic describes how prudentialization is embedded and circulates, spiraling outward through the commodity form.

It is not the case, however, that commodities communicate this risk "out of thin air." At least not initially. Commodities certainly take on this self-perpetuating and mystic attribute over time as they are increasingly fetishized (see the next section). But, even then, there is a material basis for this fetishization. For now, it is important to understand that risk thinking imbues the entire circuit of commodity production and consumption dialectically. The prudentialized commodity communicates to the market, the state, the insurance industry, the criminal justice system, the judiciary, and a wide array of regulatory systems. All potential harms to markets entail a risk calculation. Every failure is a success for risk. Over time, therefore, widgets come to increasingly represent the sedimentary effect of layer upon layer of prudential labor that is bound up in them. Indeed, prudentialism has sprung forth an industry that is as ubiquitous as knowledge itself. All of these risk calculations relentlessly orbit the billions of commodities that make up the fabric of modern insecurity, communicating risk and propelling the demand for security remedies.

Let us look at a make-believe widget factory to illustrate how this prudentialization is communicated dialectically through the commodity. A factory owner wants to make a new widget. Is it safe? Are there any foreign components? Have all of these passed inspection? How long have they been on the market? What risks do they pose to children, consumers, and the company brand? Does the assembly line need re-tooling? Does this restructuring of the work affect negotiations at collective bargaining? What types of warning labels are required? Are there any patent infringements? Does the new widget expose the company to intellectual property (IP) claims by competitors or patent trolls? Has the prototype been tested? Is it safe? How has it been received by the test group? Has the company taken adequate precautions to safeguard against industrial espionage? Is the production area secure both in terms of theft of intellectual property and real contamination that could affect the mechanisms involved? Do new security measures need to be introduced or improved in order to monitor access? For example, are personnel background checks required? Are new security technologies such as ID card readers and CCTV required? How is IT and physical security affected? Is new hardware or software required? How will the new widget affect accounting standards and internal controls? Does the production of the new widget require an environmental assessment? Are there any new exposures to federal, municipal, or state laws governing the production of the new widget? Finally, to what extent does the company wish to market the "safety" or enhanced "security" that the widget offers? After all, widgets that make people feel safer compared to competing widgets enjoy a market advantage. Not all of these risk analyses are necessary or actionable but this list is not exhaustive either. Each risk concern mobilizes its own set of interrelated assessments in relation to its own escalating expert standards[57] based on decades of related legal,[58] insurance,[59] and market liability. Remember here that the widget is *not* a security commodity per se, but its creation has launched a wide constellation of security-type labor, both in-house and contracted – making this associated, prudential labor more or less productive in capitalist terms. Of course, one may adroitly ask: would it not be so much easier if the entire production of widgets were contracted out to a place where exploitation was more intense? Where worker output was higher? Where there was a far greater institutional tolerance for risk, especially risk to workers?[60] And, of course, this is precisely what has happened in the pursuit of productive labor. But it does not entirely solve the problem of risk for the widget maker. A new series of prudential concerns arise, including intellectual property theft,[61] ensuring satellite control over craftsmanship and quality, and the emerging brand risk that, for example, "made in China" represents.[62]

To be sure, there is a very large body of scholarship that examines how this type of prudential thinking permeates contemporary institutions[63] and popular understandings[64] of risk. But what has been largely missed in all of this scholarly literature, sometimes by omission, sometimes out of a clear hostility toward Marxian orientations, [65] is that the embeddedness of security thinking has produced a type of prudential awareness that can only be achieved through mass consumerism and commodity culture. Our subjectivities, our ontological insecurities, are being increasingly shaped by how safe and secure the commodity we purchase is relative to all others regardless of how disconnected the product's actual use-value may be from security . . . at least on the face of it. Which brings us, by design, to a discussion of this commodity fetish in practice.

Fetishization

For Marx, the fetishization of a commodity relates to how the social labor that needs to be used in order to produce it becomes mystified to the user – its "secret." The commodity takes on a relationship with the consumer akin to the type of dissociation of an object and its meaning that one would see in "the mist-enveloped regions of the religious world." The more alienated from the production process workers become, the more "every product [becomes] a social hieroglyphic." Commodities lose their meaning as signaled through their actual use-value and are rather imbued with meaning entirely based on their exchange-value. For Marx, "could commodities themselves speak, they would say" that "in the eyes of each other we are nothing but exchange values."[66] Commodities thus come to be valued for reasons outside their intrinsic use. They acquire a form under capitalist mass production that divorces them from the production process in the eyes of the buyer. Imagine a time when you not only knew exactly where your shoes were made but the name of the shoemaker who crafted them. You also knew, roughly, how long it took to craft them and the level and sophistication of the craftsmanship involved. A shoe was a shoe though some shoes were better made – more durable – than others based on the materials used and the amount of labor expended in decorative leatherwork. But you did not buy a shoe because you were buying into a "lifestyle" or, except in cases of extreme affluence, because it signaled you were a certain status of person. The making of shoes was largely a local practice and was not particularly mysterious to the buyer. The price was almost entirely bound up in the materials, rent, and labor. Today, most shoe manufacturers do not actually make shoes. The lion's share of their expenditure is not spent on production at all, which they have unsurprisingly contracted out to overseas manufacturers. Klein reports that in 2000 the majority of Nike's budget was spent on marketing and advertising, not production, transport, or design.[67] When people buy shoes today, whether they are Nikes or Manolo Blahniks, they are buying brands. Brands are signifiers of distinction that now help make up who we think we are as a sort of aggregation of commodities. Treatises have been written about how these brands help make up culture itself,[68] how no matter what commodity choices we make – personal, aesthetic, political, or otherwise – we are nonetheless actively producing consumer profiles of ourselves.[69] Even the most well-meaning, purportedly anti-establishment commodity choices become part of a "rebel sell."[70]

Regardless of how these multi-layered identities are played out across race, class, and gender, the point is that the shoe like most other commodities we now consume has been fetishized. First, we really do not know, exactly, where the shoe was made, by whom, with what, over how much time, and under what conditions. This is why we watch TV programs like *How Things are Made* and why we continue to be alarmed by exposés about overseas labor conditions – we are disconnected from how these commodities come into being. This is how they first acquire their fetishistic nature. Second, as labor is increasingly pacified, made more and more *productive*, the market is flooded with increasing varieties, designs, and models of shoes. More and more money is freed up to market and advertise this increasing inventory. We are now inundated with thousands of hours of commercial advertising about the virtues of products that are, in reality, so similar that they can only be distinguished based on attributes that a century ago would seem utterly alien to us. One of these key attributes, I have argued, is the commodity's ability to communicate safety: its actual and perceived level of security.

So far we have seen that the commodification of security is characterized by its dual ability to valorize while being valorized and to prudentialize while being prudentialized. Having dealt with the fetishization of commodities in the abstract, this now begs the question: how does the commodification of security fetishize while being fetishized? So far we have said that for the commodity fetish of security to spring forth it must first be valorized and prudentialized. Put more clearly, a security commodity can only acquire its fetishistic nature once it is first made as productive as possible, manifesting as a vendible commodity (materially if possible but ephemerally if necessary). Second, the security commodity must also signal – either intrinsically in the form of the commodity's use, or extrinsically as an added method of product differentiation and status distinction through risk minimization – a sense of security. Is this product safe? Will it make me and my family safer? How secure does it make me feel when I buy it? What self-identity have I purchased? For how long? Thus, the purchase of the commodity temporarily satiates a desire for security while at the same time evoking insecurity. For now, it is important to note that completely satiating our need for security is impossible. It is a bottomless barrel of demands. How is this so? First, because the desire for security can never be satisfied physically. It is *metaphysical* want. I can certainly say "here is a security product" or "here is a product with a security feature" but I cannot ever honestly say "here is some security" and be able to ensure this. Security can never be entirely satisfied by a vendible commodity. When one considers that commodities are unceasingly broadcasting (in)security in this manner whether they are indeed security commodities or not, the social implications are profound. While the effects of this social process are surely ideological and far-reaching, it would be a mistake to assume that our analysis of (in) security ought to then focus on state discourse, international governance, military studies, and so forth – the type of thinking that dominates security studies. To be sure, since the terror attacks on New York City on September 11, 2001 entire cities became the subject of seemingly arbitrary color-coded security preparedness warnings.[71] No matter how often these warnings are satirized, security alerts have emerged permanently into public consciousness and public discourse. The threat of terrorism: Al-Qæda, the Islamic State of Iraq and Syria (ISIS), the mujahideen, and so forth amplify this sense of insecurity. All of these developments are surely important for understanding the circulation of insecurity in the capitalist world economy. But, we would be wrong to assume that 2001 somehow marked the arrival of a fetish for security – it's just empirically untrue and myopic to make such assertions. The proliferation of private security, its international consolidation, the widespread adoption of city-centre surveillance cameras, the securitization of the places and spaces where we shop, congregate, work, and play, and even the securitization of our own homes have been on the rise since the 1970s. Their seeds were planted as early as the seventeenth century. These can be traced as tangible, material changes in both the pacification of workers and the methods by which insecurities are satiated. While there can be little doubt that terror alerts amplify the general insecurity of the masses, these latest tropes of state security must not be confused as the ether in which fear and insecurity are borne. That fear and insecurity was already there, incessantly being broadcast to us by a sea of commodities that we consume on a daily basis. The fetishization of security is so ubiquitous that we now literally eat, breathe, and sleep security. Terrorism is one more consequence of this general insecurity. It may even be said that it is an *alibi*[72] for (in)security in that it both distracts us and reminds us of our own personal sense of insecurity. The fetish of security more often than not manifests itself in far more mundane and everyday commodities. As I have already mentioned, one such commodity can be as innocuous as the shoe.

A few months ago I accompanied my wife to the "Running Room"[73] – a chain retail store owned by a runner-turned-entrepeneur and set up "for runners by runners," specializing in high-end running shoes. It's the type of place you are likely to find in any bourgeois-bohemian neighbourhood. Now, there is little doubt that I am in far greater need of regular jogging regimen than my wife is but I confess I loathe the whole idea of running and, thanks to the ever-burgeoning and endlessly contradictory health pseudo-science research field, I came equipped with the latest empirical factoid indicating that running reduced one's lifespan.[74] It was clear that no one at the Running Room would be convinced, even less so coming from a middle-aged, overweight man wearing a "Star Wars" T-shirt. But I needed something upon which to base my reticence despite the eye-rolling I justifiably received in response. Just then, a stern-looking sales woman informed my partner that she needed "to learn how to run" and that her gate, as was typical for other would-be runners, "was in need of adjust-ment." Fortunately, the sales woman could help her, especially if she signed up for running classes and bought the right runner for her "type of situation." "Luckily," the sales woman added, "we have just the right type of runner for you" that, not surpris-ingly, was "a little more expensive" but well worth the cost con-sidering the devastating consequences of poor footwear on one's knees, back, and long-term health. "Whoa, that *is* fortunate," I said sarcastically. Everyone ignored my tone or pretended they didn't hear. I thought to myself: "Is she selling shoes or an entire lifestyle, a security product?" These runners would keep you safe from all sorts of injuries and, moreover, if you just let them, they would even teach you how to use them properly. The margin on the running shoe, which was priced at $200.00, must have been outrageous. But the retail-store "security sell" was just the tail-end of the circuit of production and consumption that we have already identified as part of the pacification of labor through exploitation and valorization. By now, we are all well aware of the exponen-tial rise of overseas sweat-shops where foreign workers toil for a modicum of wages to supply us with low-cost consumer goods. Were these particular Reeboks made in China by workers as young as thirteen? Did they work up to seventy-two hours a week for less than minimum wage? Did they sometimes lose fingers and hands without compensation? Were they fired if they refused overtime or became pregnant?[75] They were likely overseen by unrelenting surveillance and their movements were tracked by factory police and CCTV. The factory that produces Reeboks also makes runners for their competitors, using almost identical machinery, labor, and materials. The running shoe's intrinsic use as a shoe, how it is made, its materials, and so forth are largely secondary to its security features and the feeling one gets from donning a particular logo even though any Chinese factory worker would be hard-pressed to find any substantive difference between shoe models and brands. But these brands mean a great deal in the Running Room and to the design teams and marketers that position them in the market place. The shoe is fetishized. Its exchange-value is almost completely divorced from its use: $2.30 worth of pacified labor and shipping with $200.00 worth of "vibe," marketing, and "value-added" point-of-sale pitch. The whole process, however, has been colored by a compulsion for security – right from the immizerated Chinese factory worker, to the high-seas freight and dock-workers, to the slick, commission-based sales staff and right to the uncertain buyer worried that they ought to purchase the right shoe to ensure against injury. After all, what's your health really worth to you? "If you don't have your health, what do you have?" the sales girl asked.

But even this is not the whole story. Running shoes have, at least since the 1980s and the advent of the Air Jordan sneakers, been part of status-seeking associated with their own risks. The progressive criminologist Elliot Currie in his general theory of the culture of "market violence" specifically cited the act of "rolling" someone for their running shoes as a key indicator of the phenomenon of youth valuing things over people.[76] Only recently, another teen was shot for a pair of vintage Air Jordans in Texas.[77] The running shoe, therefore, is at the same time a risk calculation and a commodity for status attainment. It signals security. Only a few weeks after we bought the Reeboks, my wife was asked to remove them at the airport. Thanks to Richard Reid, the infamous "shoe bomber" who tried to blow up an American Airlines flight only two months after the attacks on 9/11, adults now must remove their footwear for inspection before being allowed on to a plane. I watched the Reeboks rattle along the conveyor belt and into the scanner as a security officer looked intently at an outline on a view screen. The magical Reeboks were, like all other shoes, now also a potential weapon of mass destruction. Of course, we diligently removed our shoes despite the fact that we knew that the entire process was nonsense. It has become ritualistic. Children can keep their shoes on. No liquids or gels over 100mL and no more than three bottles. Everybody senses that these rules are arbitrary. They were spoofed and ridiculed almost as soon as they were announced,[78] yet more than a decade later we are still taking our shoes off. Can terrorists not simply combine liquids or gels on the plane? Are suicidal terrorists really beyond using children? It didn't matter. We abided to get on the plane, queuing in what any extraterrestrial would rightly confuse with a religious procession replete with offerings to the security machine for blessing. So we watch our shoes, belts, laptops, tablets, and carry-on bags enter "the mist-enveloped regions of the religious world,"[79] where none of these objects are taken at their use. The commodities, along with the passengers to whom they belong, manifest only as a security concern.

Now, I want to be clear here that the shoe is no special commodity under capitalism. In fact, there are far better examples of fetishized commodities than the running shoe to illustrate the fetish of security. These include the wide array of security products and features associated with automobiles, personal devices, appliances, home and office safety, online social media, and even products such as life banks[80] and identity-theft insurance.[81] The list goes on. My point, however, is to make clear that the ubiquity of both commodity fetishism and security impacts all corners of production and consumption in a capitalist economy. As I will explain in the next chapter, this ubiquity means that security has become hegemony. But before we move on, let us recap how the fetishization of security manifests itself *materially* in the commodity form:

1. We are alienated from the production of commodities as we ourselves are commodified. Their production becomes mysterious to us, losing their use-value relative to their relational exchange-value. They become 'social hieroglyphics' increasingly signaling insecurity.

2. The interpenetration of the security commodity and commodities in general through the valorization and prudentialization process increasingly imbues all commodities with security meanings.

3. The mass proliferation of commodities in a world capitalist economy facilitates the mass proliferation of insecurity as security becomes a marker of distinction embedded in the commodity.

4. Because every new, upgraded, commodity signals the previous commodity's failure, its obsolescence, our consumer culture is based on a generalized insecurity where the attainment of more security is a marker of status distinction.

Now, these four facets of the fetishization of the security commodity relate to crucial aspects of the production process, and, more specifically, how labor is deployed, alienated, and valorized eliciting this fetish. The implications of the rise of the security commodity for the social world are thus potentially profound. Consider that if Marx was right that security is "the supreme concept of bourgeois society" just as the commodity is "the elementary form of wealth" then what is the effect of the fetishization of the security commodity on the social world? In the next chapter the political, theoretical, and social implications of this contemporary confluence is examined further, culminating in a materially grounded argument that security is not just becoming hegemonic, it *is* hegemony.

Notes

1. Fyodor I. Kushnirsky, and J. Stull William, "Productive and unproductive labour: Smith, Marx, and the Soviets," in *Perspectives on the History of Economic Thought*, ed. Donald A. Walker (Aldershot: Gower, 1989), pp. 82–103 ; Patricia Ewick, "Corporate cures: The commodification of social control," *Studies in Law, Politics, and Society* 13 (1993): 137–57.

2. Indeed, the RCMP employs 100 employees to actively manage their brand, generating 2.5 to 3 million dollars in licensing fees for the RCMP Foundation. See: Douglas Quan, "Despite the Bad Press, the

Rcmp Brand Is Still 'Strong'," *Ottawa Citizen* (2012), <http://www.ottawacitizen.com/entertainment/Despite+press+RCMP+brand+still+strong/6864084/story.html> (accessed October 2015).

3. The barcodes were also affixed to public spaces like the back of street signs whenever Intelligarde's contracts required them to patrol outdoors. Sometimes this would be on public land, as in the case of Toronto's Port Authority or Parking Authority. From the point of view of security, the city was carved up into private patrol grids.

4. Karl Marx, *Capital, I* (New York: Penguin, 1976a), Ch. 25, "The general law of capitalist accumulation," pp. 304–12.

5. Karl Marx, *Capital, III*, trans. Ben Fowkes (New York: Penguin, 1976b [1867]), Chs 13–15 "The falling rate of profit," pp. 339–48.

6. Karl Marx, *Capital, III*, trans. Ben Fowkes (New York: Penguin, 1976b [1867]), Part III "The law of the tendency of the rate of profit to fall," pp. 317–78.

7. Trevor Jones, and Tim Newburn, *Private Security and Public Policing* (New York: Oxford University Press/Clarendon, 1998); Nigel South, *Policing for Profit* (London: Sage, 1988); Les Johnston, *The Rebirth of Private Policing* (London: Routledge, 1992); George S. Rigakos, *The New Parapolice: Risk Markets and Commodified Social Control* (Toronto: University of Toronto Press, 2002).

8. C. D. Shearing and Jennifer Wood, *Imagining Security* (London: Willan Publishing, 2006); David. H. Bayley, and Clifford Shearing, "The future of policing," *Law and Society Review* 30(3): 585–606; Clifford D. Shearing, and Philip C. Stenning, "Private security: Implications for social control," *Social Problems* 30(5) (1983): 498–505; Richard V. Ericson, and Kevin D. Haggerty, *Policing the Risk Society* (Toronto: University of Toronto Press, 1997).

9. George S. Rigakos, "Beyond public–private: Toward a new typology of policing," pp. 260–319 in *Re-Imagining Policing in Canada*, ed. Dennis Cooley (Toronto: University of Toronto Press, 2005); Mark Neocleous, and George S. Rigakos, "Anti-security: A declaration," pp. 15–21 in *Anti-Security* (Ottawa: Red Quill Books, 2011).

10. George S. Rigakos, "The significance of economic trends for the future of police and security," pp. 176–9 in *Police and Security: What the Future Holds*, ed. Jane Richardson (Ottawa: Canadian Association of Chiefs of Police, 2000); J. Kakalik, and S. Wildhorn, "Private police in the United States," (Washington, DC: Government Printing Office, 1971).

11. Thomas Piketty, *Capital in the Twenty-First Century* (Cambridge,

MA: Belknap Press, 2014); Richard D. Wolff, "The Keynesian revival: a Marxian critique," pp. 103–14 in *Saving Global Capitalism: Interrogating Austerity and Working Class Resoonses to Crises*, eds Carlo Fanelli, Chris Hurl, Priscillia Lefebvre, and Gulden Ozcan (Ottawa: Red Quill Books, 2011).

12. W. C. Cunningham, J. J. Strauchs, and C. W. Van Meter, *Private Security Trends 1970–2000: The Hallcrest II* (MacLean: Hallcrest Systems Inc., 1990).

13. Karen Swol, "Private security and public policing in Canada," pp. 15–25 in *The Juristat Reader* (Toronto: Thompson Educational Publishing, 1999); Trevor Sanders, *Rise of the Rent-a-Cop* (Ottawa: Law Commission of Canada, 2003).

14. Trevor Jones, and Tim Newburn, *Private Security and Public Policing* (New York: Oxford University Press/Clarendon, 1998).

15. Volker Eick, "Preventive urban discipline: Rent-a-cops and neo-liberal glocalization in Germany," *Social Justice* 33(3) (2006): 1–19.

16. George S. Rigakos, and Georgios Papanicolau, "The political economy of Greek policing: Between neo-liberalism and the sovereign state," *Policing and Society* 13(3) (2003): 271–304.

17. Maria Los, and Andrew Zybertowicz, *Privatizing the Police State: The Case of Poland* (New York: St. Martin's Press, 2000).

18. Ronald van Steden, *Privatizing Policing: Describing and Explaining the Growth of Private Security* (Amsterdam: Boom Juridische Uitgevers, 2007).

19. Jaap de Waard, "The private security industry in international perspective," *European Journal on Criminal Policy and Research* 7 (1999): 143–74.

20. For countries where such longitudinal data has been available.

21. Maria Los, "Lustration and truth claims: Unfinished revolutions in Central Europe," *Law and Social Inquiry* 20 (1995): 117.

22. Vadim Volkov, *Violent Entrepreneurs: The Use of Force in the Making of Russian Capitalism* (Ithaca: Cornell University Press, 2002).

23. Alfried Schulte-Bockholt, "A Neo-Marxist explanation of organized crime," *Critical Criminology* 10(3) (2004): 225–42.

24. (ADS Sicherheit Group, Top Control Group), Hungary (Bantech Security Rt.), Austria (SOS), Finland (SPAC), Czech Republic (BOS: Bankovi Ochranna Sluzba, a.s.), France (OGS, EuroGuard), Poland (BRE Services), and Norway (Unikey AS). These acquisitions were

quite large. EuroGuard employed 4,200, ADS 1,200, and BOS 1,200.

25. Immediately after the takeover, two regional market leaders were also acquired in the US: First security Corp. and American Protective Services Inc. This was followed by the purchase of Smith Security Inc., Doyle Protective Service Inc., and APG Security. In 2000, Securitas acquired Burns, thus making it a major player in the largest security market in the world overnight. In 2001, Securitas bought Loomis Amored car, a company with more than 220 offices across the United States, employing another 2,200 officers.

26. For example: Rigakos, *The New Parapolice: Risk Markets and Commodified Social Control*; Clifford D. Shearing, and Philip C. Stenning, "Reframing policing," pp. 9–18 in *Private Policing*, eds Clifford D. Shearing and Philip C. Stenning (Newbury Park: Sage, 1987a); Bayley and Shearing, "The future of policing"; Jones, and Newburn, *Private Security and Public Policing*; Johnston, *The Rebirth of Private Policing*; George S. Rigakos, *Nightclub: Bouncers, Risk and the Spectacle of Consumption* (Montreal: McGill-Queen's University Press, 2008); Mark Button, *Security Officers and Policing: Powers, Culture and Control in the Governance of Private Space* (Aldershot: Ashgate, 2007); Alison Wakefield, *Selling Security: The Private Policing of Public Space* (Devon: Willan Publishing, 2003).

27. Cunningham, Strauchs, and Van Meter, *Private Security Trends 1970–2000: The Hallcrest II*.

28. "Hyperpanoptics as commodity: The case of the parapolice," *Canadian Journal of Sociology* 23(1) (1999): 381–409.

29. Rigakos, *The New Parapolice: Risk Markets and Commodified Social Control*.

30. Rigakos, "Hyperpanoptics as commodity: The case of the parapolice."

31. Ibid.; Rigakos, *The New Parapolice: Risk Markets and Commodified Social Control*.

32. Andy Dawson, "Robot security guard is a cross between R2-D2 and Wall-E's girlfriend," in *Mirror.com* (2014), London: Daily Mirror, <http://www.mirror.co.uk/news/technology-science/technology/robot-security-guard-cross-between-4622495>.

33. "Knightscope autonomous data machines," <http://knightscope.com/technology.html> (accessed November 2015)

34. David F. Noble, *Forces of Production: A Social History of Industrial Automation* (New York: Oxford University Press, 1986).

35. Richard W. Hadden, *On the Shoulders of Merchants: Exchange and*

the Mathematical Conception of Nature in Early Modern Europe, Suny Series in Science, Technology, and Society (Albany: State University of New York Press, 1994).

36. George S. Rigakos, "On continuity, risk and political economy: A response to O'Malley," *Theoretical Criminology* 5(1) (2001): 93–100.

37. Ian Hacking, *The Emergence of Probability* (Cambridge: Cambridge University Press, 1975).

38. Ian Hacking, *The Taming of Chance*, Ideas in Context (Cambridge and New York: Cambridge University Press, 1990).

39. H. A. L. Cockerell, and Edwin Green, *The British Insurance Business, 1547–1970* (London: Heinemann Educational, 1976), p. 4.

40. Mark Greengrass, "English projectors and contingency planning in the later seventeenth century," Herzog August Bibliothek, Wolfenbüttel: Paper presented at Publicists and Projectors in Seventeenth-Century Europe Conference, 1996, p. 2, my emphasis.

41. James Franklin, *The Science of Conjecture: Evidence and Probability before Pascal* (Baltimore: Johns Hopkins University Press, 2001).

42. Edwin Black, *IBM and the Holocaust: The Strategic Alliance between Nazi Germany and America's Most Powerful Corporation*, 1st edn (New York: Crown Publishers, 2001).

43. Oscar H. Gandy, *The Panoptic Sort: A Political Economy of Personal Information* (Boulder: Westview Press, 1993).

44. Nils Christie, "Suitable enemies," pp. 42–54 in *Abolitionism: Toward a Non-Repressive Approach to Crime*, eds H. Bianchi and R. Van Swaaningen (Amsterdam: Free University Press, 1986).

45. Linda Hunt, *Secret Agenda: The United States Government, Nazi Scientists, and Project Paperclip, 1945 to 1990*, 1st edn (New York: St Martin's Press, 1991).

46. Michael Lewis, *Moneyball: The Art of Winning an Unfair Game*, 1st edn (New York: W. W. Norton, 2003).

47. Michael Lewis, *Flash Boys: A Wall Street Revolt*, 1st edn (New York: W. W. Norton and Company, 2014).

48. Ulrich Beck, *Risk Society: Towards a New Modernity*, trans. Mark Ritter (London: Sage, 1992), p. 36; Ulrich Beck, *World Risk Society* (Malden: Polity Press, 1999).

49. Anthony Giddens, *Modernity and Self-Identity: Self and Society in the Late Modern Age* (Cambridge: Polity Press, 1991).

50. Zygmunt Bauman, *Postmodernity and Its Discontents* (Cambridge: Polity, 1997).

51. Frank Furedi, *Culture of Fear: Risk Taking and the Morality of Low Expectation* (Harrison: Continuum Publications, 1997).

52. Neil Postman, *Amusing Ourselves to Death: Public Discourse in the Age of Show Business* (New York: Viking, 1985).

53. Richard V. Ericson, Kevin D. Haggerty, and Kevin D. Carriere, "Community policing as communications policing," pp. 37–70 in *Community Policing: Comparative Aspects of Community Oriented Police Work*, eds Dieter Dölling and Thomas Feltes (Holzkirchen: Felix-Verlag, 1993).

54. Aaron Doyle, and Richard Ericson, *Uncertain Business: Risk, Insurance and the Limits of Knowledge* (Toronto: University of Toronto Press, 2004); Richard V. Ericson, *Crime in an Insecure World* (Cambridge: Polity Press, 2007).

55. Pat O'Malley, "Legal networks and domestic security," *Studies in Law, Politics, and Society* 11 (1991): 171–90.

56. Rigakos, *The New Parapolice: Risk Markets and Commodified Social Control*, p. 25.

57. Robert Castel, "From 'dangerousness' to risk," pp. 281–98 in *The Foucault Effect: Studies in Governmentality*, eds Graham Burchell, Colin Gordon, and Peter Miller (Chicago: University of Chicago Press, 1991).

58. George L. Priest, "The new legal structure of risk control," *Daedulus* 119 (1990): 207–27.

59. Francois Ewald, "Insurance and risk," pp. 197–210 in *The Foucault Effect: Studies in Governmentality*, eds Graham Burchell, Colin Gordon, and Peter Miller (Chicago: University of Chicago Press, 1991).

60. Paul Kellogg, "Goodbye to the working class?" *IS* 36(2) (1987): 108–10.

61. Carl A. Roper, *Trade Secret Theft, Industrial Espionage, and the China Threat* (Boca Raton: CRC Press, 2014).

62. Paul Midler, *Poorly Made in China: An Insider's Account of the Tactics behind China's Production Game* (Hoboken: Wiley, 2009).

63 For a decent review I recommend: Hazel Kemshall, *Understanding Risk in Criminal Justice* (Berkshire: Open University Press, 2003); Gabe Mythen, *Ulrich Beck a Critical Introduction to the Risk Society* (London: Pluto Press, 2004); David Garland, "The rise of risk," pp. 48–86 in *Risk and Morality*, eds Richard V. Ericson, and Aaron Doyle (Toronto: University of Toronto Press).

64. Kevin Haggerty, "From risks to precaution: The rationalities of personal crime convention," pp. 193–214 in *Risk and Morality*, eds

Richard Ericson, and Aaron Doyle (Toronto: University of Toronto Press, 2003); Alan Hunt, "Risk and everyday life," pp. 165–92 in *Risk and Morality*, eds Richard Ericson, and Aaron Doyle (Toronto: University of Toronto Press, 2003).

65. In this regard, see the illustrative exchange between Pat O'Malley and Hadden & Rigakos: Rigakos and Hadden, "Crime, capitalism and the risk society: Towards the same olde modernity?" *Theoretical Criminology* 5(1) (2001): 61–84; Pat O'Malley, "Discontinuity, government and risk: A response to Rigakos and Hadden," *Theoretical Criminology* 5(1) (2001): 85–92; George S. Rigakos, "On continuity, risk and political economy: A response to O'Malley," *Theoretical Criminology* 5(1) (2001): 93–100.

66. Marx, *Capital, I*, Section 4 "The Fetishism of Commodities and the Secret Thereof", p. 53.

67. Naomi Klein, *No Logo: Taking Aim at the Brand Bullies* (Toronto: Vintage Canada, 2000), p. 11, Table 1.1, and pp. 16–26.

68. Mary Douglas and Baron Isherwood, *The World of Goods: Towards an Anthropology of Consumption* (New York: Routledge, 1996 [1979]); Jean Baudrillard, *The Consumer Society: Myths and Structures*, trans. Chris Turner (Thousand Oaks: Sage, 1998 [1970]).

69. Oscar H. Gandy, *The Panoptic Sort: A Political Economy of Personal Information* (Boulder: Westview Press, 1993).

70. Joseph Heath and Andrew Potter, *The Rebel Sell: Why the Culture Can't Be Jammed* (Toronto: HarperPerrenial, 2005).

71. "Homeland Security Advisory System," Wikipedia entry, <http://en.wikipedia.org/wiki/Homeland_Security_Advisory_System> (accessed November 2015).

72. Jean Baudrillard, *Simulations* (New York: Semiotext(e), 1983).

73. Running Room, <https://www.runningroom.com/hm> (accessed November 2015).

74. McGinn, Dave, "Another study says that too much running is bad for you, but there's more to the story," *Globe and Mail*, February 4, 2015, <http://www.theglobeandmail.com/life/health-and-fitness/fitness/why-again-study-that-says-too-much-running-is-bad-is-too-good-to-be-true/article22782320>

75. *Business Week*, March 2000, p. 45. See also, generally: Klein, *No Logo: Taking Aim at the Brand Bullies*.

76. Elliot Currie, "Market, crime and community: Toward a mid-range theory of post-industrial violence," *Theoretical Criminology: An International Journal* 1(2) (1997): 147–72.

77. KHOU staff news, "Craigs List ad for Air Jordans leads to arrest over stolen car," April 7, 2015, <http://www.khou.com/story/news/crime/2015/04/07/craigslist-ad-for-air-jordans-leads-to-shooting-arrest-over-stolen-car/25398633> (accessed November 2015).

78. If you have not seen it yet, you must see the spoof on Saturday Night Live: "Security refresher on liquid gels," Saturday Night Live, November 24, 2010, <http://www.funnyordie.com/videos/24fc3124ab/homeland-security-refresher-on-liquids-and-gels-snl> (accessed November 2015).

79. Marx, *Capital*, *I*, Section 4 "The Fetishism of Commodities and the Secret Thereof", 53.

80. Lifebank, <http://www.lifebank.com> (accessed November 2015).

81. Mayer, Andre, "Identity theft insurance: Is it worth it?" *CBC News*, January 21, <http://www.cbc.ca/news/business/identity-theft-insurance-is-it-worth-it-1.2919364> (accessed November 2015).

5 Security is Hegemony

If you would like to get a quick sense of how ubiquitous security-thinking has become in our everyday lives, I can recommend a couple of social experiments. At your next celebration where bringing a gift is the anticipated social norm, take the intended recipient aside and as you hand them their present, politely warn them, "I just need to let you know, this item does not meet established safety standards." Note the recipient's reaction. This is particularly effective when you are not well known to the recipient (although I would not recommend it, especially if the recipient is a parent accepting the present on behalf of a child). Here's another statement that can be used to great effect, particularly in Ottawa where many of the people I meet through friends and acquaintances work for the federal government. After saying hello and asking the obligatory, "And where do you work?" respond to their job title with the following: "Oh, I could never work there. I would never qualify for the security clearance." Or, you can substitute: "I'd never pass the background check." It usually has the same effect: awkward silence or a quick change of topic. Indeed, perhaps the only other intentional security-related faux pas that seems to surpass both of these statements is to say outright, "I am against security." (It helps to maintain a dead-pan expression and offer no follow-up explanation.) The point here is not to be the designated social pariah at future social events but rather, even if you never try these social experiments yourself, to think about the meaning of the responses you would likely receive. Like other, far more sophisticated experiments in social psychology, the point is to bring to light a part of the human condition that is otherwise unseen or misunderstood. It is, in this case, to scrutinize the power of the ideology of security.[1] We are bombarded with all sorts of security indicators today that signal to us safety, social status, inclusion, and desirability in a manner that would be utterly alien to previous generations. Our security mindset has been conditioned by the myriad institutions we come into contact with on a daily basis and by our making and consumption of commodities: the security–industrial complex. As Foucault would put it, we self-discipline ourselves based on a set of institutional demands that seek to assess and categorize us.[2] Our security status is now our master status. This is the existing ether in which we accede to social norms, institutional demands, and the scope of politics. It is where we come to know what we know.

How ideology works to pressure and perpetuate a particular social order and what it may take to break through and upend a dominant ideology has been the subject of numerous works by a wide array of intellectuals, radicals, and social activists. These recipes for eliciting revolutionary breaks vary considerably, of course, and include the radical democratization of the electoral and political process;[3] the timing of political[4] and economic conjunctures[5] that create openings for radical intervention; the performance of everyday situational protest;[6] armed guerilla insurrection;[7] a vanguard workers' party;[8] direct action;[9] national liberation from colonial practice;[10] non-violent, passive resistance;[11] and social movement activism.[12] All of these perspectives – in one way or another – have some built-in analysis about why things remain the way they are and how they may be changed. Thus, while bourgeois "society must be defended"[13] against whatever revolutionary alternative is being hatched, the task is to overcome this edifice. What maintains the capitalist state, therefore, is the existence of an ideological architecture that "manufactures consent"[14] and that must be analysed and overcome if the purported revolution is to move forward. Two influential Marxist thinkers in this regard are Louis Althusser and Antonio Gramsci. Although they have often been juxtaposed to each other, their ideas can be read as complementary. Gramsci is known for his analysis of hegemony, and Althusser, in part as response to Gramsci's theory, for his contribution to an analysis of ideology.

For Althusser,[15] what becomes possible in terms of our roles and prospects is pre-structured by social practices that are tied to institutional frameworks. These frames he divides into two types: the Repressive State Apparatus comprised of police, courts, and prisons and the Institutional State Apparatus that consists of family, religious institutions, the media, and the education system. When Althusser attempted to explain how ideology works in everyday practice, how it comes to constitute individual consciousness, he offered the example of a police officer hailing a person on the street. Responding to a simple shout of, "Hey, you there," the resultant act of turning around to see what is the matter transforms that person into a subject. For Althusser, the larger point is that the individual's awareness of this subjectivity is always already part of the existing ideology. By virtue of the pre-existing rules, structures, and institutions we are born into, ideology conditions what is possible, even in terms of who we think we are and can be in any number of potential situations.

Gramsci similarly emphasized the role of consciousness, especially in education, in his notion of cultural hegemony, arguing that "these various categories of traditional intellectuals . . . put themselves forward as autonomous and independent of the dominant social group,"[16] although quite clearly for Gramsci they do little other than reinforce the existing system. These "men of letters" become dependents and thus proponents of a system that allows them to act as simple orators. In Gramsci's view, cultural hegemony is reflected in how ruling elites continue to win the consent over those whom they exercise power. Of course, the task once again becomes overcoming, circumventing, and defeating this hegemony as part of revolutionary struggle. This attempt to understand the success of your enemy has been at the heart of the notion of hegemony since its first modern use in plotting opposition to the Russian Tsar.[17] For Day,[18] hegemony remains a dominant concept among radical thinkers, undermining the Left's ability to grasp the potential of the new social movements that eschew attempts to impose a pre-figured, programmatic change. Yet we know that state and ruling elites collude, plan, and reinforce the ideological status quo. This cannot be ignored by progressive thinkers either. As Lebowitz[19] points out: "the absence of a vision of a socialist alternative ensures that there is no alternative to capitalism. If you don't know where you want to go, no road will take you there." In the absence of programmatic change, protest is hard pressed to galvanize political opposition, as was evidenced during the Occupy movement. All that remains, therefore, is for the analyst to draw some tired conclusions about how relatively autonomous state institutions are from the needs of economic elites and how permeable the capitalist state is to counter-hegemonic politics.[20] But these are all variations on a theme that seem to bypass or downplay the most prescient aspects of ideology and hegemony: the central role of security.

Both Althusser and Gramsci aimed to understand the resilience of the capitalist order despite repeated crises. Both of their approaches, however, can also be read as symptomatic of the general deficit of existing radical theory. The security of the order, while central to understanding the system's endurance, hardly figures into their revolutionary analyses. It is as if security were taken for granted and its fabrication accepted as obvious. Security becomes a dependent aside to the machinations of a broader politics at a grander level of political economy rather than the central motor for its preservation. When both Althusser and Gramsci make secondary the idea of security in their analyses, they are following a script long established within the Left of security's relegation to an instrumental notion of power such that security is merely what *we* shall use when *we* are in power – a new, counter-hegemonic power to be magically unsheathed by a righteous ruling authority. As if the Left were to free Excalibur from its stone. Gramsci's and Althusser's analyses are also symptomatic of further deficits of radical politics. They not only fail to see the importance of security for hegemony and ideology but divorce it from any materialist grounding. There is no consideration of value creation, of the basic economics of security. They thus ignore the industry of security except in a most spurious way. Finally, when these considerations are absent, two fundamental problems of the Left are further reinforced: (1) a radical theorization of security is never developed; and (2) no programmatic ideas about security after capitalism are entertained. Together, this highlights the problem of the absence of a police science among progressives.

Yet Gramsci and Althusser are also largely correct so far as their analyses take them. The modern capitalist system has a created a colossal mechanism for, as Herman and Chomsky later put it, "manufacturing consent,"[21] and this can indeed be analysed through an understanding of everyday ideology as well as the institutional forms that defend and reinforce this hegemony. There is, of course, considerable conceptual slippage between these ideas of hegemony versus ideology and so it is worthwhile for us to set down how these notions are distinct yet complimentary. *Ideology is a perpetual state of being wherein we come to read the existing social order and our place within it at any given time. Hegemony is the process by which state and corporate institutions perpetuate and defend this dominant ideology.* Both ideology and hegemony, however, *are overwritten by security.* First, by the very basic material reality that security is but the modern institutional manifestation of our built-in survival instinct and, second, and relatedly, by virtue of the fact that, as we have seen, security is inscribed in the commodity form through valorization, prudentialization, and fetishization. This is why to say "I am against security" is such a radical statement. It signals an opposition to the entire global economic system and is a repudiation of the institutions that defend it. It is counter-hegemonic because in *literal terms* it counters the entirety of hegemony. It does so because the hegemony is made up of ideological forms, constituted by the commodity that signals a need, lack, or fear – a deficit of security. This process can be described in an even simpler way. A political economy wherein the commodity broadcasts insecurity through the entire circuit of production to consumption, globally reinforces security and fuels its cyclical and insatiable demand. This is why security *is* hegemony. It is ubiquitous, far-reaching, and the final arbiter in all social transactions from cocktail parties to global crises.

To say that security is hegemony, however, is not to say that doing security is merely some sort of narrowing and/or superimposition over all aspects of human relations. It is more than this. The nature by which security overwrites both hegemony and ideology is evidenced in the everyday practices of production, consumption, and reproduction. Effortlessly used in verb, noun, and adjective forms, the idea of security grafts itself easily on to almost any social problem. Take, for example, the burgeoning area of "food security." Food security, as Neocleous points out,[22] has emerged as a new and powerful discursive terrain. There are numerous international conferences on food security that bring together security experts, agribusiness experts, foreign relations experts, military experts, and, of course, development experts. There are new journals devoted entirely to this idea. And, in principle, why would anyone be opposed to food security? It is indeed a broad church that attracts all sorts of thinkers from a wide array of disciplines and branches of government, non-governmental organizations (NGOs), and academia. Food security, after all, seeks to maintain supply chains, offset crises, minimize shortages caused by climate change, and even mitigate against the risk of political upheaval that may result. But what we now call food security used to be called "world hunger" with a very different political intent and dynamic. Food security begs the question "whose security?" and transmutes a general altruistic human desire to feed one's neighbor into a logistical, risk calculation now institutionally overwritten by security concerns. All sorts of experts from a wide swath of society are invited to participate. Local "stakeholders" are sought after rather than excluded. Their potential opposition is accepted and the information they have to offer is considered invaluable. Whatever information they offer, however, in the end is digested as *security intelligence* in one branch of the global security nexus circumscribed within the possibilities of a capitalist world economy. An economy that must be secured, often against the social and environmental crises it created.

My own work is no different. It can also be read as security intelligence. I have seen first-hand how what I would have considered a radical intervention is interpreted as part of my standing as an expert, offering one more bit of useful information. My research on bouncers and the productive aspects of masculine violence in the nighttime economy turned me into an expert on nightclub safety.[23] My research on the rise of the aggressive *parapolicing*[24] turned me into an expert on the boundaries between public and private security provision. In both instances, I was legally accepted as an expert by a judge, my testimony bounded by the facts and my knowledge rendered useful. So, it is clear that security-talk does something quite significant to the understanding of social consequences that the system it seeks to preserve often creates in the first place. This is surely security's linguistic power and at the root of its ability to colonize so many types of political discussions. But it would be wrong to interpret this as a narrowing of discourse. The success of the hegemony of security, especially at institutions like universities and, of course, military and strategic think-tanks is precisely because it is open to information based on its "usefulness," its ability in potentially fabricating a state of security. Security, in fact, has become so ubiquitous and embedded within the fabrication of society and economy that we ought to start addressing how it may not just be preeminently reproductive hegemonically but also materially *productive* within capitalism.

Notes

1. Stephen Spitzer, "Security and control in capitalist societies: The fetishism of security and the secret thereof," pp. 43–58 in *Transcarceration: Essays in the Sociology of Social Control*, eds John Lowman, Robert J. Menzies, and Ted S. Palys (Aldershot: Gower, 1987).

2. Michel Foucault, *Discipline and Punish* (New York: Vintage Books, 1977); Michel Foucault, "Governmentality," pp. 87–104 in *The Foucault Effect: Studies in Governmentality*, eds Graham Burchell, Colin Gordon, and Peter Miller (Chicago: University of Chicago Press, 1991).

3. C. B. Macpherson, *The Life and Times of Liberal Democracy* (Oxford: Oxford University Press, 1977).

4. Louis Althusser, *For Marx*, trans. B. R. Brewster (London: Verso, 1997 [1969]); Vladimir I. Lenin, "What is to be done? Burning questions of our movement," pp. 347–530 in *Lenin Collected Works*, vol. 5 (Moscow: Foreign Languages Publishing Press, 1961).

5. Ernest Mandel, *Long Waves of Capitalist Development: A Marxist Interpretation* (London: Verso, 1995 [1980]).

6. Ken Knabb, *Situationist International Anthology* (Berkeley: Bureau of Public Secrets, 1981).

7. Ernesto Guevara, *Guerrilla Warfare* (Harmondsworth: Penguin, 1961).

8. Lenin, "What is to be done? Burning questions of our movement."

9. David Graeber, *Direct Action: An Ethnography* (Oakland: AK Press, 2008).

10. Vladimir I. Lenin, *Imperialism, the Highest Stage of Capitalism* (Peking: Foreign Languages Press (1975 [1952])); Frantz Fanon, *The Wretched of the Earth* (New York: Grove P, 1963).

11. Leo Tolstoy, Leo Wiener, and Paul Avrich Collection (Library of Congress), *The Kingdom of God is Within you; or, Christianity Not as a Mystical Teaching but as a New Concept of Life* (New York: Noonday Press, 1961).

12. Ernesto Laclau and Chantal Mouffe, *Hegemony and Socialist Strategy: Towards a Radical Democratic Politics*, trans Winston Moore and Paul Cammack (London: Verso, 1985).

13. Michel Foucault, *"Society Must Be Defended": Lectures at the Collège de France, 1975–1976*, trans. David Macey (New York: Picador, 2003).

14. Edward S. Herman and Noam Chomsky, *Manufacturing Consent: The Political Economy of the Mass Media* (New York: Pantheon Books, 1988).

15. Louis Althusser, "Ideology and Ideological State Apparatuses (notes toward an investigation)," trans. Ben Brewster, pp. 127–86 in *Lenin and Philosophy and Other Essays*, ed. Louis Althusser (New York: Monthly Review Press, 1971).

16. Antonio Gramsci, *Selections from Prison Notebooks* (London: New Left Books, 1971), pp. 7–8.

17. See Perry Anderson, "The antinomies of Antonio Gramsci," *New Left Review* (Nov–Dec 1976): 5–78. The concept of "gegemoniya" was first deployed by Plekhanov and Axelrod against Tsarist absolutism. The idea was then taken up by Lenin in *Reformism in the Russian Social-Democratic Movement* where the hegemony of the Tsar was to be upended by another: "The proletariat is revolutionary only in so far as it is conscious of and gives effect to this idea of the hegemony [gegemoniya] of the proletariat" (see Vladimir I. Lenin, "Reformism in the social democratic movement," trans. Dora Cox, pp. 229–41 in *Lenin Collected Works*, vol. 17 (Moscow: Progress Publishers, 1974), pp. 232–3. Lenin was restating the case for a vanguard worker's party to lead the way (Lenin, "What is to be done? Burning questions of our movement.")

18. Richard J. F. Day, *Gramsci Is Dead: Anarchist Currents in the Newest Social Movements* (Toronto: Between the Lines, 2005).

19. Michael Lebowitz, *The Contradictions of "Real Socialism": The Conductor and the Conducted* (New York: Monthly Review Press, 2012).

20. Nicos Poulantzas, "The capitalist state: A reply to Miliband and Laclau," *New Left Review* (Jan–Feb 1976), pp. 63–83; Ralph Miliband, "Poulantzas and the capitalist state," *New Left Review* (Nov–Dec 1973), pp. 83–92; Ralph Miliband, "The capitalist state: Reply to N. Poulantzas," *New Left Review* (Jan–Feb 1970), pp. 53–60; Nicos Poulantzas, "The problem of the capitalist state," *New Left Review* (Nov–Dec 1969), pp. 63–78.

21. Herman and Chomsky, *Manufacturing Consent: The Political Economy of the Mass Media.*

22. Neocleous, *Critique of Security.*

23. Rigakos, *Nightclub: Bouncers, Risk and the Spectacle of Consumption.*

24. Rigakos, *The New Parapolice: Risk Markets and Commodified Social Control.*

6 The Productivity of Security

In late January of 2015, I hosted a talk at Carleton University in Ottawa, Ontario, delivered by Jeff Halper, an internationally recognized activist-scholar based out of Israel. He was visiting Ottawa on a fund-raising tour and I was meeting him for the first time. Halper is the founder of the Israeli Committee Against House Demolitions (ICAHD) and a Nobel Peace Prize nominee. I quickly came to like him. Short, stocky, white-bearded, and affable, Jeff delivered an impactful and well-researched presentation about the Israeli security–industrial complex. His talk was based on his forthcoming book[1] that examined how Israel "strategically niche-fills the contours of the world's arms and security industries" and, moreover, on how the Israeli state's continuing "securocratic" order may be understood within the context of a capitalist world-system based on pacification. A colleague in my Department aptly summarized his presentation as equally "enlightening and terrifying."

Yet, despite the power of his talk, one point kept gnawing at me. Why was it that despite decades of domination into all facets of Palestinian life, the Israeli state had found no way of making the Palestinians productive? In fact, contrary to what pacification theory would suggest, the Israeli securocratic order had shown a clear disinterest in fostering any productive activities in the occupied territories. Yet the key elements were there: violent and relentless dispossession; the obliteration of means of self-sufficiency; and the exercise of military and policing domination. Still, there was no tangible evidence that the Israelis cared much about extracting any surplus-value from the Palestinians. Were they a particularly poor example of colonial rule? Where was the commodification of labor and the intensification of work? Certainly, there were small-scale examples here and there. Cheap, security-vetted Palestinian laborers were allowed to work in Israel but, of course, were not permitted to vote. Small shops did produce some goods, often as coops organized by women. But clearly these projects did not come close to addressing the overriding motor of pacification as I have described it: the exploitation of labor; the making of productive subjects. This had been a matter of some concern for me both theoretically and politically as the Left tried to take stock of the capitalist order in the wake of the Great Recession of 2008. It seemed that everywhere pacification was ramping up as talk of austerity for the poor and welfare for wealthy bankers and traders had taken hold. Reiman's old Marxist assertion that "the rich get richer and the poor get prison"[2] seemed more adroit than ever.

Indeed, by the beginning of 2009, the global financial crisis – spawned by banking liquidity shortfalls, reckless mortgage lending, shady financial products, short-sighted deregulation, rising oil prices, and a massive expansion in US household debt – had turned into the worst worldwide recession since 1930. Massive state bail-outs had already been issued. The US Federal Reserve, the European Central Bank, and other central banks around the world purchased $2.5 trillion of government and private assets to prop up private lending institutions. European governments and the United States also back-filled the capital of their national banks by $1.5 trillion, purchasing newly issued preferred stock in major domestic chartered banks. Stimulus packages in the trillions soon followed in an attempt to stop a deflationary spiral caused by a loss of available credit and record unemployment. It was by far the largest combined international monetary action in world history[3] and Keynsianism,[4] at least for the banks, appeared to have returned with a vengeance.[5] As governments tried to decide what firms would have to be salvaged, what companies could be sacrificed, what sectors would be kept afloat, and how many jobs could be created, a tired, long-forgotten concept that pre-dated Keynes by more than a century, but that had preoccupied me for the last five years, crept back into the lexicon of bourgeois economics: *productive* labor.

In late February 2009, the editors of *The Economist* stepped into a political firestorm stoked by news of grotesque executive compensation packages, the rapid decline of manufacturing jobs, and growing taxpayer outrage and alienation. The magazine's editors pleaded for governments, particularly the US government, to make *rational* policy decisions based on strategic investments in the economy. Although conceding that "[n]ext to scheming bankers, factory workers look positively deserving" the *Economist's* editors nonetheless argued that no special consideration should be given to manufacturing. Instead, they argued: "[t]he important distinction is not between manufacturing and services, but between *productive and unproductive* jobs."[6] That such a labor distinction was invoked in *The Economist,* a magazine that is widely considered an international bastion of conservative economic wisdom, is indeed remarkable. After all, the productive–unproductive distinction is a notion long rejected[7] by mainstream economists.[8] Even more surprising was that the editors were deploying this distinction during a crucial turning point in world history, not merely as an analytic abstraction but as the material basis for determining the distribution of government resources at the height of the Great Recession. As a basis for state intervention, such economic thinking had not been mobilized since the demise of the Soviet National Accounting System. In the end, the editors actually got the distinction quite wrong[9] but, at least for a brief time, productive labor was once again up for discussion.

"Perhaps Israel was an exception" I conceded to Jeff Halper as we chatted in my office after his talk. He was not as convinced about Israel's exceptionalism as he was about about Israel's niched role in the global "matrix of control," as he called it. We were joined in my office by Jeff's hosts in Ottawa who were understandably eager to get him off to his next stop.[10] "Maybe the Israelis simply cannot risk promoting industry of any kind," I thought aloud. "They probably fear it could help finance Palestinian resistance." But this concern seemed unsatisfying to the both of us. Domestic resistance is presupposed by pacification and is as historically commonplace as imperialism itself. Every imperial force has had to deal with this same problem. Fortunately, we had enough time to think through the productivity issue together until the blatantly obvious finally dawned on us. What if the "Palestinian problem" *itself* was productive? Palestinians had become the experimental subjects for a wide slew of military and security hardware that Israeli industries exported all over the world. This industry was certainly productive. Halper had convincingly documented that the issue of the Palestinian problem was now the basis of a highly profitable industry. The Palestinian issue not only reinforced the Israeli state through constant insecurity, it supported a deeply interpenetrating series of private-state syndicates ranging from drone technologists to terror risk assessment analysts to VIP protection trainers to tiny spywear engineers through to classic weapons manufacturers of the well-known Uzi submachine gun and the Galil assault rifle. It is, after all, a $15 billion a year industry comprising up to 8.5 per cent of Israel's gross domestic product (GDP).[11]

If you have been following what has been covered in the preceding chapters, the idea that security may be productive hardly amounts to a breakthrough assertion at this point of the book. Indeed, that security can be productive seems to follow from all that has been covered so far. As production is more alienating and mysterious, commodities become social hieroglyphs that signal insecurity. These commodities (in general) and security commodities (specifically) interpenetrate each other, imbuing all commodity exchange with security meanings. The mass proliferation of commodities results in the mass proliferation of security considerations communicated at each moment of exchange. Each upgrade signals insecurity that reestablishes the demand for security cyclically. The ubiquity and reach of security thus becomes hegemonic as it is broadcast through both the circuits of commodity production and consumption becoming essential to the maintenance of political, legal, and economic structures. Thus, a consideration of whether security is productive or not merely reminds us of the assertion we arrived at in Chapter 1: attempting to catalog, fix, and measure what is notionally blurred, transitional, and fluid under capitalism – the transformation of labor through the pacification process – is distracting and inherently unachievable. Security may be productive or may not be. This depends on whether surplus-value is being extracted. This is what we have called the economic catalyst for pacification. But what if pacification can be made productive even when it fails? Even when little or no surplus-value can be directly extracted from subject populations? Even when there is no accumulation through exploitation? Would this mean that those pacified, by virtue of simply being pacified, are productive? Is the Palestinian militant hiding under urban rubble, therefore, just as productive for the Israeli security–industrial complex as the Israeli laborer fabricating the electronics necessary to potentially kill or maim him? By acceding to this possibility we would be arguing that pacification itself can be productive; that pacification does not only seek to fabricate a productive subject but, failing this, that pacification can be a productive enterprise on its own.

Suggesting that the security–industrial complex can be productive certainly fits with what we have argued thus far but it runs contrary to both Smith's and Marx's formulations. In fact, both of these giants of political economy argued unequivocally that security was certainly not productive. Smith argued that the "sovereign ... with all the officers *both of justice and war* who serve under him," including "the whole army and navy, are unproductive labourers." Why? Because

> [t]hey are the servants of the public, and are maintained by a part of the annual produce of the industry of other people. Their service, how honourable, how useful, or how necessary soever, produces nothing for which an equal quantity of service can afterwards be procured. The protection, security, and defence of the commonwealth, the effect of their labour this year will not purchase its protection, security, and defence for the year to come.[12]

When Marx, too, considered the productivity of security he agreed with Smith and mocked latter-day nineteenth-century economists who sought to reimagine as productive the continuation and expansion of unproductive labor that, with the decline of feudalism, now acted at the behest of capitalist interests. Suddenly, priests, soldiers, and civil servants were being reclaimed as productive workers. Marx answers these attempts to re-classify and the needs they are ostensibly addressing as supposedly productive in the following way:

> It can just as well be said that illness produces physicians, stupidity produces professors and writers, lack of taste poets and painters, immorality moralists, superstition preachers and *general insecurity produces the sovereign.* This way of saying in fact that all these activities, these services, produce a real or imaginary use-value is repeated by later writers in order to prove that they are productive workers in Smith's sense, that is to say, that they directly produce not products *sui generis* but products of material labour and consequently immediate wealth.[13]

As we have already argued, Marx, like Smith before him, took great delight in capitalism's denigration of those "noble professions" that he equated to the productive equivalent of "clowns or menial servants." He mocked the idea that all forms of human activity led to economic value:

> The criminal produces not only crimes but also criminal law, and with this also the professor who gives lectures on criminal law and in addition to this the inevitable compendium in which the same professor throws his lectures on the general market as "commodities."[14]

To be clear, Marx was arguing that crimes and criminals just like illness, stupidity, lack of taste, immorality, superstition, and insecurity, should certainly *not* be considered productive and that the resultant commodity produced could not be attributed to the criminal's supposed productivity. In the same manner, Marx would likely argue that the Palestinian militant and the "Palestinian problem" are certainly not productive. It is unclear whether Marx believed the professor who produces his "inevitable compendium" as a result of criminal activity was productive but, once again, we ought to not get bogged down in these determinations because we have already arrived at the general tenet that *labor in its ideal bourgeois form wants to create surplus value through material commodity production.* Thus, there is no reason why within contemporary capitalist economies security cannot be productive depending, of course, on how it is configured. In fact, we have argued that all indications are that security is increasingly becoming an essential component of the productive economy. To be fair to both Marx and Smith, it would have taken a monumental leap of imagination in the late eighteenth century and early nineteenth to predict that security would be configured in this manner: that vendible security commodities would be so ubiquitous; that even general commodities were apt to broadcast insecurity. Security, at that moment of capitalist development, was indeed almost exclusively[15] an unproductive state function.

Yet the legacy of Marx's dismissal of the productivity of security has had a profound influence on the Left. Marx, himself, did not consider the role of security in his labor theory of value, nor in his history of economics, nor as anything more than a supreme *concept* of bourgeois society. The result is that a consideration of the material, economic role of security is completely missing in latter Marxian formulations largely because it was barely mentioned in Marx's general critique of political economy. So, while examples of pacification and the use of violence through dispossession, exploitation, and the valorization of labor abound throughout Marx's work, these historical examples do not figure in any prominent way in his cyclical theory of capitalism nor, especially, in his consideration of the countervailing tendencies of capital to stave off collapse. More specifically, Marx's prediction of the rate of profit to decline leading to a potential system-wide failure of the capitalist economy contains no consideration of the resultant role, effect, and countervailing forces that this crisis could mobilize in the form of security. Marx could not have foreseen that security would be embedded within the commodity itself. After all, in the nineteenth century, security was more or less, as Foucault would later describe it, a ceremonial and external manifestation of state power. Of course, we are now in a position to appreciate that security is far more robust and materially integrated within late capitalism,[16] from the content of the commodity form through to the sociopolitical reproduction of global, hegemonic capitalist relations. In fact, my recent empirical work with co-author Aysegul Ergul has shown that the increased pacification of subject populations is far more prevalent where there are higher rates of insecurity. Both across national divides[17] and over time,[18] employment in the public and private protective services climbs with increasing inequality. In fact, it seems as though public and private policing employment marches in lockstep with increasing rates of inequality.

In considering the productivity of security, therefore, we must examine both how this manifests at the level of the commodity as well as the capitalist system writ large. For example, how may the productivity of security embody itself in the doing of security labor? Beginning with the grander political economy of epochal shifts of production we seem to go from tribal rotation, to feudal obligation, to public duty and then security enterprise. Security labor has successively become more and more alienated. In the end, we have the core embodiment of the security aesthetic under late capitalism in its commodified form: a contract security guard working for a multinational organization at the behest of a corporate client unrelated to the guard's own home and family, working strange hours, conducting patrols that are under constant surveillance so that the guard's immaterial labor may be representationally transformed into a vendible form. The security guard is the security product. Emblazoned with a corporate log, a shoulder patch sets the guard apart – a patch to which the security worker has almost no meaningful allegiance or connection. It has to be one of the most alienating forms of labor developed and yet it represents the most "productive" manifestation of security next to new vendible commodities such as CCTV cameras and even robot guards that are already replacing the worker, making this security labor even more insecure.

Previous considerations of unproductive labor have looked at what happens when this sector of the economy continues to grow while the proportion of productive labor continues to decline. This is an idea I introduced in Chapter 1 but that now needs to be revisited. Remember that there was a time when Marxist scholars considered this productive–unproductive dynamic central to understanding the likelihood and timing of the revolution and even the identification of potential allies. Becker even suggested that the collapse of empires could be linked to the unchecked growth of unproductive labor.[19] He cites the case of Egyptian high priests whose increasingly ritualistic drain on the proceeds of the slave-based economy and their growing size and power eventually contributed to a system-wide collapse. Their unproductive labor could no longer be supported. In a similar way, we may surmise that as the manufacturing of "vendible commodities" decreases and as unproductive service sector employment (including both state and private security) increases in an effort to soak up over-production and the increased size of the surplus population (in part, thrown out of work by increased mechanization), this will inevitably result in systemic collapse. As I have already mentioned, such a thesis on the growth of unproductive labor suffers from at least three analytic problems. The first problem is that, as we have seen, it is often quite difficult to definitively categorize a wide gamut of work within late capitalism as either productive or unproductive. Notwithstanding that we have arrived at a clear understanding of what productive labor looks like in its ideal bourgeois form, outside this formation the gradations nonetheless seem endless and we are still without an acceptable method for assigning workers to either group. The second problem is that there is no way of knowing when we have reached the limit of unproductive labor. What is too much unproductive labor? No one knows what minimum proportion of the economy must be involved in the classic sense of producing vendible commodities to sustain the whole. This is, of course, compounded by the first problem where it is almost impossible to easily identify this ratio in the first place. Finally, in a global capitalist economy it makes very little sense to talk of the decline of productive labor, particularly as when we lament post-industrialism in North America all the while industrialism flourishes in Asia.[20] Thus, the third problem we tend to suffer from is taking this national data out of an international context. With these three provisos in mind, we can now add yet another: that what was formerly considered an unproductive albeit necessary aspect of capital accumulation may in fact be potentially productive. Thus, at a more macroeconomic level, this means that simply pacifying a population can be an industry in itself. A pacification with no end – with no chance of real security. Security becomes its own industry divorced from a solution. This malleability of security value as we have described it, this fetishistic quality in the commodity, allows for the productive creation of insecurity not only as a political tactic, for this has always been the case across various epochs, but as an industrial maneuver aimed at profit-making. It is surely rent-seeking in the historic sense but also now an intrinsic part of the sustainable ebb and flow of capitalism. This means that the very elements that buttress and save the state from periodic crises are, in fact, not an unfortunate drag on capitalism but rather essential for its longevity in a far more profound and embedded way than was previously appreciated.[21]

Contrary to previous assumptions, security does not make capitalism "moribund"[22] but rather is integral to its growth and revitalization. It is important that the political gravity of this argument not be overlooked. If security can be productive then the fabrication of an inherently insecure order does not challenge that order, for the preservation of order is an industry in itself. This is qualitatively different than the defense of every other mode of production that has preceded capitalism. We simply cannot say that the economic spin-offs of enforcing pacification, beyond the economic ends of extracting surplus from subject populations, were ever previously productive in this way. Only under the global capitalist economy and the rise of the modern security–industrial complex has this been possible. Security technology has become so ubiquitous and has penetrated so widely into all facets of human exchange – from the supra-national mobilization of security forces to the individual choice between competing security-infused commodities – that it is now an embedded and productive aspect of the entire system. The defining characteristic of capitalism, therefore, is its ability to productively sell (in) security to those it makes insecure. In effect, to sell the poison of pacification as cure. By successfully doing so it staves off its own extinction in a manner that no other mode of production has ever been able to accomplish. Capitalism will thus reign supreme so long as this cycle of pacification continues to churn.

Notes

1. Jeff Halper, *War against the People: Israel, the Palestinians and Global Pacification* (London: Pluto Press, 2015), p. 1.
2. Jefferey Reiman, *The Rich Get Richer and the Poor Get Prison* (Needham Heights: Allyn and Bacon, 1995).
3. Roger Altman, "The Great Crash, 2008: A geopolitical setback for the West," *Foreign Affairs* 88(1) (2009), <http://www.for eignaffairs.com/articles/united-states/2009-01-01/great-crash-08> (accessed October 2015).
4. John Maynard Keynes, *The General Theory of Employment, Interest and Money* (Cambridge: Cambridge University Press, 1936).
5. Robert J. Skidelsky, *Keynes: The Return of the Master* (New York: Public Affairs, 2009).
6. *The Economist*, February 21; my emphasis.
7. This is part and parcel of modern economics' rejection of political economy and the labor theory of value.
8. George Stigler, "The success and failures of Professor Smith," *Journal of Political Economy* 84(6) (1976): 1,199–213.
9. They had forsaken not only Karl Marx's but also Adam Smith's original definition of productive labor. For both Marx and Smith, manufacturing labor was, of course, productive labor par excellence. No matter, however, as the editors' true motivation was likely propping up and excusing finance capital at the expense of manufacturing. Given the prevailing political, economic, and regulatory climate, the editors of *The Economist* took the middle ground. They bypassed the wisdom of Smith, Keynes, and, not surprisingly, Marx in favour of inaugurating a monthly column in the name of Joseph Schumpeter whom they celebrated as a "champion of innovation and entrepreneurship." Thus, the return to vogue of Milton Keynes was only one of many great returns. Marx's *Capital* and Smith's *Wealth of Nations* – seminal economic treatises that only weeks before collected dust on library and bookstore shelves – were now in hot demand. Economists, policy-makers, and intellectuals had momentarily – albeit only rhetorically – turned their backs on neo-liberalism and had begun scrambling through the classics in search of forgotten conceptual tools to understand a very modern financial disaster.
10. Including Peter Larson who is Chair of the National Education Committee on Israel Palestine and by a representative from the

First Unitarian Church of Ottawa where he was scheduled to speak next.

11. From Halper, *War against the People*. He cites INSS (The Institute for National Security Studies), Strategic Survey for Israel, 2014–2015, 2015, pp. 170–1. Retrieved at: <http://www.inss.org.il/uploadImages/systemFiles/INSS2014-15Balance_ENG%20(2).pdf> (accessed November 2015); SIPRI, *Background Paper on SIPRI Military Expenditure Data, 2011*, 2012. Retrieved at: <http://www.sipri.org/media/pressreleases/press-release-translations-2012bgeng.pdf> (accessed November 2015).

12. Adam Smith, *The Wealth of Nations* (New York: Random House, 1937 [1776]), Part II.3.2; my emphasis.

13. Karl Marx, *Theories of Surplus-Value, III*, trans. Jack Cohen (London: Lawrence and Wishart, 1972b), Chapter IV, p. 410; my emphasis.

14. Karl Marx, *Grundrisse*, trans. Martin Nicolaus (New York: Penguin, 1973), p. 378.

15. There were, of course, private policing experiments taking place in the English context in the early 1800s, including the Thames Police, the Bow Street Runners, and various shady underworld characters such as the "thieftaker general" Jonathan Wild who worked both sides of the law. But these were eventually overtaken by a centralized, salaried police service based out of Scotland Yard in 1830: a system akin to the state-centred policing already well established on the Continent. For an excellent comparative historical account consult: Clive Emsley, *The English Police : A Political and Social History, 2ed.* (New York: Harvester Wheatsheaf, St Martin's Press, 1991); Clive Emsley, "A typology of nineteenth century police," *Deviance et Societe* 3(1) (1999b): 29–44; Clive Emsley, *Gendarmes and the State in Nineteenth-Century Europe* (Oxford: Oxford University Press, 1999a). For a historiographic review, particularly of the role of private policing and thief-taking, consult: John L. McMullan, "The new improved monied police: Reform, crime control, and the commodification of policing in London," *British Journal of Criminology* 36(1) (1996): 85–108; John L. McMullan, "Social surveillance and the rise of the 'police machine'," *Theoretical Criminology* 2(1) (1998): 93–117.

16. Ernest Mandel, *Late Capitalsim* (London: NLB, 1975).

17. George S. Rigakos, and Aysegul Ergul, "Policing the industrial reserve army: An international stud," *Crime, Law and Social Change* 56(4) (2011): 329–71.

18. George S. Rigakos, and Aysegul Ergul, "The pacification of the American working class: A longitudinal study," *Socialist Studies* 9(2) (2013): 167–98.
19. James F. Becker, *Marxian Political Economy: An Outline* (Cambridge: Cambridge University Press, 1977).
20. Paul Kellogg, "Goodbye to the working class?" *IS* 36(2) (1987): 108–10.
21. Vladimir I. Lenin, *Imperialism, the Highest Stage of Capitalism* (Peking: Foreign Languages Press, 1975 [1952]).
22. Stephen Spitzer, "Security and control in capitalist societies: The fetishism of security and the secret thereof," pp. 43–58 in *Transcarceration: Essays in the Sociology of Social Control*, eds John Lowman, Robert J. Menzies, and Ted S. Palys (Aldershot: Gower, 1987).

Conclusions: Security after Capitalism

In mid-November of 2014, my friend and colleague Georgios Papanicolaou and I participated in a unique meeting of radicals, academics, police executives, and police union leaders in Athens, Greece. The three-day workshop was organized by the Nicos Poulantzas Institute[1] and the Rosa Luxemburg Foundation[2] and funded by Transform Europe![3]: a pan-European network set up by the coalition of the radical left in the EU parliament. The theme of the workshop was "Democratizing the Police in Europe with a Particular Emphasis on Greece." This was also the title of the policy paper Georgios and I had written and it served as the focal point of discussion for the gathering.[4] The Nicos Poulantzas Institute was by now well recognized by the European Left as the think-tank and policy laboratory of Greece's emerging Syriza party. A political party that a few months later would ride its anti-austerity platform, its strong grass-roots mobilization of the working class, and its outright rejection of the established oligarchical parties of the Centre-Right New Democracy (ND) and the Centre-Left Pan-Hellenic Socialist Movement (PASOK), to a historic victory in the 2015 election that January. But already in November the prospects for a Syriza government were looking promising. Polls were indicating that the Greek electorate was fed up with widespread government corruption and a never-ending national debt and recession. Voters were also angry that their own politicians had almost bankrupted the country, stole hundreds of millions of Euros, and turned over the future of the nation to the "Troika" (European Central Bank, International Monetary Fund, and European Commission) of Eurocrats and banksters.

There was now a palpable energy on the streets of Athens. It felt to all like we were on the cusp of a historic change to both Greek and European politics, and perhaps even to the nature of the EU itself. Yet despite all of this hope a dark cloud still loomed ominously on the political horizon. It was a familiar cloud that workshop attendees, from war-weary communists to old-guard police, were all too familiar with. It was, in fact, Greece's new Finance Minister Yiannis Varoufakis who would later more aptly describe this gathering cloud as the coalescing of Greece's "dark forces."[5] These dark forces were perhaps more obvious in Athens than in other European capitals but as Georgios and I explained at the workshop, these domestic forces were an extension of a global security–industrial complex that had as its central goal the pacification of workers, pseudo-colonial subjects, radicals, and, of course, anything or anyone that pushed back against the fabrication of a capitalist world order. In Greece, the extreme Right Golden Dawn party was also on the rise, from fringe group with no real hope of parliamentary representation to Greece's third largest party only two months later. Golden Dawn had infiltrated the Hellenic Police and attacked foreigners and anarchists while the police looked on.[6] Their anti-Euro position, xenophobia, and isolationism had struck a chord with a portion of the Greek population.

For the first time, however, Syriza and the European Left were taking security seriously. They knew that the old instrumentalist understanding of police power had to be rethought, especially as prospects for the first bona fide radical Left party in Europe since the French Revolution was taking shape. As the workshop wound down we dined with a former high-ranking officer of the Hellenic Police. The Taverna was only blocks away from where university student Alex Grigoropoulos was shot and killed by police in 2008, igniting riots throughout Greece and Europe. Exarcheia, Athens' anarchist district, was a fitting backdrop for our discussion. It represented both the hopes and frustrations of Greece's youth. It was also, not coincidentally, a stronghold of Syriza support. In 2008, Syriza had unequivocally condemned the killing of Grigoropoulos as a "cruel murder" rallying anarchists and the wrath of the police. As we made our way to dinner we strolled past anarchist graffiti and a wall mural that memorialized

Grigoropoulos. At dinner, our police companion chronicled the alarming rise of Golden Dawn in frightening detail. At first, Golden Dawn was relegated to backwater and remote island outposts on the Greek periphery. "When they started infiltrating the officer ranks of the Greek police HQ" he lamented "I had to get out. I had lost hope." But then he paused, smiled, and added: "But if I were still there today I think I would stay." He continued: "Today there is hope." It was as clear to us then as it is now: Syriza would not just be an experiment in anti-austerity and democracrtic governance. It would be an experiment in how a new, hopeful, and progressive social order can be brought into existence. Time will only tell whether Syriza survives, whether it will help build a "new Europe," and reform Greece's state institutions by rooting out clientalism and widespread tax evasion. It also remains to be seen whether Syriza will be overwhelmed by the "dark forces" that stand ready to benefit from draconian international forces that would seek "regime change"[7] in Athens or even Greece's exit from the European Union.[8] Whatever the case may be, the problem of social order for a bona fide Leftist government remains a pressing concern. It is, in my opinion, the lynch-pin for all transformative efforts.

But how *does* a leftist government, as in the case of Greece, best preside over those same agencies that were complicit with occupation forces during Second World War and served British and American imperial interests afterwards? Indeed, many of the same radicals who made up the core of Syriza's "Left Platform" had been arrested and even tortured during the reign of the military junta of the colonels (1967–74). Yet, here we all were. In one room. Talking about the future of security. I don't think I'll ever experience anything quite like it again in my lifetime. Georgios and I took our turn, making our case for a Left policy on security. We were arguing for more than the removal of fascist elements from the police; the disbanding of the paramilitary protest police units that hunkered down in buses outside Syntagma Square only blocks from our meeting room; the establishment of community foot patrols; new training and oversight standards; outreach with immigrant groups; and the inclusion of the Hellenic Police union into the general union movement. We were certainly proposing all of these initiatives (and more) as did many others in attendance. But beyond these direct and important reforms we were also suggesting something more important to the future prospects of not only Syriza and radical Left parties across Europe but the Left in general. A new police science. Indeed a socialist police science that would commit itself to the technical aspects of fabricating a new social order. A social order that, much like the capitalist police science before it, took seriously the legal, economic, and security planning necessary for the transition from one mode of production to another. Police science did not view security as its enemy. It understood that pacification through exploitation, through dispossession, was essential for making capitalism possible. A theory of doing violence was part of every economic plan, every "emprovement," every colonization, every urban reform. Resistance was always anticipated. For this very reason, a new police science is a very hard sell to progressives of all political affinities. Greece, replete with geopolitical tensions and its history of internal civil strife, is not unique in this regard. As Papanicolaou and I pointed out, the problem is that there has never been an alternative police science for an alternative social and economic order. While a prescriptive formulation for a system of social control seems unthinkable, even abhorrent for most revolutionaries today, as Harvey has argued, "One of the problems with lately lamented communism is that it didn't ask these questions about everyday life." It did not seriously query "what would a transition out of capitalism to socialism look like?" I agree with Harvey when he says that this "plays a critical role in thinking about any revolutionary process."[9] As a consequence, Papanicolaou and I argued that "radical democratic governments are unprepared to deal with the police because they have not applied themselves to a serious examination of policing and its potential place in a new participatory economy."[10] What happens in the absence of such a comprehensive examination?

Just imagine what the world would look like if the security–industrial complex remains unchallenged and unchecked by the potential for an alternative system. A complex that is not only integrated with capital but fuels its ideological and material foundation, acting for capital's expansion, self-preservation, and renewal.

Imagine a system of totalizing risk management, surveillance, and exploitation: an incessant (in)security. It would be a system that would operate at the highest echelons of global financial capital and sovereignty, exacting "fiscal waterboarding"[11] on non-compliant states. Its ubiquity would reach the lowest and deceptively frivolous rungs of loss prevention at Disney World,[12] denying entry to those who do not submit to electronic fingerprinting. It would be embedded into all facets of human interaction. This type of social science fiction is not so hard to fathom at all. We are already there. The dream of this contemporary "police machine" is complete telematic awareness.[13] A system wherein nothing escapes the scope of pacification. Where the certainty of mass surveillance[14] covers us in a fog of trepidation and risk aversion. We become the system's subjects and products, busily managing our profiles in repetitive acts of self-discipline that come to condition our everyday existence. The ideological and hegemonic consequences, as we have seen, are quite profound. Within such a system, every form of resistance is already prudentially pre-calculated. It is built into commodity production and the control and maintenance of workers. Even loafing – that primitive attempt by workers to steal back labor-time – has already been calibrated into the system. There is no real cheating. Cameras, production quotas, and new Taylorizing algorithms come to dominate all facets of the worker's life. All, of course, in the pursuit of profit and the concentration of capital and power. A digital panopticon that would make Bentham envious and Colquhoun marvel.

An alternative to this mass pacification is needed. A post-capitalist future depends on systematically re-purposing this apparatus and harnessing its technological potential for a democratic security at the core of a democratic economic social order. We must not await some "inevitable" crisis of overproduction, nor pine for the right revolutionary balance of productive and unproductive workers, nor the magic of some historic conjuncture. The task at hand is to plan. It ought to be in the form of implementing a painless police science that transitions us from capitalism to a new democratic, global economic system. We know that such a seemingly grandiose transition is doable because it has been done before. Capitalism has been fabricated through security.

While security is more pervasive, networked, and all-consuming than it has ever been, it has also become far more vulnerable and susceptible to penetration. The redesign of security thus makes the redesign of society writ large far easier than the original Enlightenment era police scientists could have ever imagined. We are fast approaching a point where our global society, now so integrated and co-dependent with the systems of pacification that subtend it, may be reconfigured through a mere re-write of the security code at its core. The planning for such a future ought to begin in earnest. Security structures need to be reimagined and there are already cracks showing. A counter-hegemonic, anti-security in various forms is making an impact. But we cannot simply wish away these structures either. While we may indeed *re*produce them, how we act upon and within these structures reifies them in the process. Structures cannot be changed by merely thinking differently about them in some constructivist sense. We need to be unapologetically and scientifically realist. Which is certainly not the same as being *politically* realist in a limiting sense. We need to continue to identify and analyse "human drives and activities behind the abstract forces that structure the capitalist system,"[15] including those drives that condition us to seek out security in a vulnerable, isolating trap.[16] These drives can only be momentarily satiated through the consumption of more commodities, more (in) security. If, as we have said, security is not only ideologically and economically reproductive but increasingly productive in its own right then we would be wise to begin with undermining the creation of surplus value at the motor source for all other exploitative relations. Security must be socialized, not in some generic sense but literally by undermining any capitalist enterprises that make profit off of human misery and subjugation. To start, we must get our structures right. The security–industrial complex goes beyond the prison–industrial complex,[17] the entrepreneurial aspects of the crime control industry,[18] the military–industrial complex,[19] and even the wide-ranging, taxonomical research undertaken as surveillance studies.[20] The security–industrial complex is, materially and ideologically, the blast furnace of global capitalism, fuelling both the conditions for the system's perpetuation while feeding relentlessly on the surpluses it has exacted. Without an alternate security model the complex will continue to feed itself and resuscitate capitalism. It is the ultimate countervailing tendency hiding in plain view. We cannot know when the revolution will come but we can be certain that it will be broadcast as a security crisis: the last fitful sputtering of a doomed economic order being re-written from the inside.

Six months after Syriza's stunning electoral victory I was having lunch with a colleague who was attending Ottawa for the annual Congress meetings. A sociologist of Greek descent, she is an expert on diaspora studies and particularly the experiences of immigrant women. We exchanged updates on our research and I told her about my work on theorizing pacification and, of course, we talked about developments in Greece. It was the type of discussion that progressives were having the world over. Could Tsipras achieve a restructuring? What do you make of Varoufakis? What would happen to Syriza under intense pressure from the Germans? Should Greece exit the Euro and reintroduce the drachma? Austerity, everyone could clearly see, was hitting the most vulnerable, the most insecure, the hardest.

"Do you know," she shared "in Piraeus, where my mother is from, an older widow we know well, a pensioner, depends on the neighborhood free markets set up by Syriza sympathizers to distribute food." The markets were organized by left-wing activist networks formed in response to the crisis produced by austerity. They collected, sometimes cajoled, and sometimes guilted, regional growers into donating some of their produce to the most needy. The continued existence of these markets was both sad and reassuring. It was heart-warming to hear about such important solidarity efforts. It was also the type of organized, community effort that helped solidify Syriza's popular support among the poor and helped vault them into a political force in Greece.

"But the old woman is afraid," she continued. "She's afraid of going to the market. She's scared of the youth, the unemployed, the migrant foreigners she does not know. She doesn't want to be mugged again. They already took her bag once. She's quite scared." There were indeed reports that the police had pulled back on their patrols, that the new Syriza government did not want a renewal of conflicts with marginalized groups. The police had acquired a well-deserved reputation of heavy-handed, often violent responses and for routinely hassling immigrant youth under the previous conservative government.[21] A renewal of such conflicts would likely be embarrassing to Greece's new government.

Yet, if this state of affairs was not emblematic enough of the Left's failure to offer an alternative form of security, she continued: "She's frail, so she calls for an escort. And she's not the only one. It's quite common in that area for the elderly."

"But do you know *who* she calls?" she asked me rhetorically. "She calls the local Golden Dawn office. They send over two 'palikarya,'[22] as she calls them, in black shirts to escort her to and from the market. They take her by the arm and watch over her the whole way there and back. They even help her carry her groceries." She paused, watching me shake my head in amazement, and finally added, "George, the woman raves about them."

I cannot imagine a more telling portrait of the Left's failure to think through the revolutionary significance of security nor a more fitting way to reinforce the central political entreaty of this book. In the heart of crisis-ridden Greece, at the ostensible birthplace of democracy, under the nose of an ostensibly radical-Left government, two neo-Nazis proudly escort one of society's most vulnerable members to a community free market. A market run by new social movement activists whose organization and commitment helped build the solidarity necessary to produce Europe's first radical Left government in generations. No account could better encapsulate the need for a new police science than the stark political reality of this image. It highlights the obvious intellectual disconnect between police and economy that continues to plague progressive thinking.

Notes

1. See <http://poulantzas.gr> (accessed November 2015).
2. See <http://www.rosalux.de/english/foundation.html> (accessed November 2015).
3. See <http://www.transform-network.net/home.html> (accessed November 2015).

4. Georgios Papanicolaou, and George S. Rigakos, "Democratizing the police in Europe with a particular emphasis on Greece," Athens: Nicos Poulantzas Institute and Transform! European Network, 2014.

5. Georgios Papanicolaou and George S. Rigakos, "Golden Dawn and the 'Dark Forces'," *Jacobin Magazine*, February 24, 2015, <https://http://www.jacobinmag.com/2015/02/greece-syriza-police-reform> (accessed October 2015).

6. Amnesty International, *A Law unto Themselves: A Culture of Abuse and Impunity in the Greek Police* (London: Amnesty International Publications, 2014).

7. Seumas Milne, "Syriza Can't Just Cave In. Europe's Elites Want Regime Change in Greece," *The Guardian,* 2015, <http://www.theguardian.com/commentisfree/2015/jul/01/syriza-cave-in-elites-regime-change> (accessed November 2015).

8. Julia Amalia Heyer, Fiona Ehlers, Horand Knaup, Peter Müller, Ralf Neukirch, René Pfister, Christoph Schult, and Timo Steppat,"A government divided: Schäuble's push for Grexit puts Merkel on defensive," *Speigel Online*, 17 July 2015: <http://www.spiegel.de/international/germany/schaeuble-pushed-for-a-grexit-and-backed-merkel-into-a-corner-a-1044259.html> (accessed October 2015).

9. See Harvey's online lectures on Capital, especially *Chapter 15: Machinery and Large-Scale Industry, Sections 1–3*, <http://davidharvey.org/2008/08/marxs-capital-class-08> (accessed November 2015).

10. Georgios Papanicolaou, and George S. Rigakos, "Democratizing the police in Europe with a particular emphasis on Greece," Athens: Nicos Poulantzas Institute and Transform! European Network, 2014.

11. Reprinted English version of interview with *Republicca* of Greek finance minister Yiannis Varoufakis. See <http://yanisvaroufakis.eu/2015/01/05/stop-greeces-fiscal-waterboarding-interviewed-by-la-repubblica> (accessed November 2015).

12. Clifford D. Shearing, and Philip C. Stenning, "SAY 'CHEESE:' The Disney order that is not so Mickey Mouse," pp. 317–23 in *Private Policing*, eds Clifford D. Shearing and Philip C. Stenning (Newbury Park: Sage, 1987b).

13. William Bogard, *The Simulation of Surveillance: Hypercontrol in Telematic Societies* (Cambridge: Cambridge University Press, 1996).

14. Glenn Greenwald, *No Place to Hide: Edward Snowden, the N.S.A., and the U.S. Surveillance State* (New York: Metropolitan Books, 2014).

15. Steve Hall, and Simon Winlow, *Revitalizing Criminological Theory: Towards a New Ultra-realism* (Abingdon: Routledge, 2015), p. 130.

16. Steve Hall, Simon Winlow, and Craig Ancrum, *Criminal Identities and Consumer Culture* (Collumpton: Willan, 2008).

17. Christian Parenti, *The Soft Cage. Surveillance in America: From Slave Passes to the War on Terror* (New York: Basic Books, 2003).

18. N. Christie, *Crime Control as Industry* (London: Routledge, 1993).

19. Jeff Halper, *War against the People: Israel, the Palestinians and Global Pacification* (London: Pluto Press, 2015); Peter B. Kraska (ed.), *Militarising the American Criminal Justice System: The Changing Roles of the Armed Forces and the Police* (Boston: Northeastern University Press, 2001).

20. David Lyon, *The Electronic Eye: The Rise of Surveillance Society* (Minneapolis: University of Minnesota Press, 1994).

21. Amnesty International, *A Law unto Themselves: A Culture of Abuse and Impunity in the Greek Police.*

22. In this context, palikarya means "strong," "young Greek men," or "strapping lads" akin to "tall and sturd."

Bibliography

Adams, Howard. 1975. *Prison of Grass: Canada from the Native Point of View*. Toronto: New Press.

Adams, James Truslow. 1984. *Provincial Society, 1690–1763*. Westport: Greenwood Press.

Albritton, Robert. 2007. *Economics Transformed: Discovering the Brilliance of Marx*. Ann Arbor: Pluto Press.

Althusser, Louis. 1971. "Ideology and Ideological State Apparatuses (notes toward an investigation)." Trans. Ben Brewster. Pp. 127–86 in *Lenin and Philosophy and Other Essays*, ed. Althusser, Louis. New York: Monthly Review Press.

Althusser, Louis. 1997 [1969]. *For Marx*. London: Verso.

St Altman, Roger. 2009. "The Great Crash, 2008: A geopolitical setback for the West." *Foreign Affairs* 88(1) (2009): <http://www.foreignaffairs.com/articles/united-states/2009-01-01/great-crash-08> (accessed October 2015).

Amnesty International. 2014. *A Law unto Themselves: A Culture of Abuse and Impunity in the Greek Police*. London: Amnesty International Publications.

Anderson, Perry. 1976. "The antinomies of Antonio Gramsci." *New Left Review* (Nov–Dec): 5–78.

Baudrillard, Jean. 1983. *Simulations*. New York: Semiotext(e).

Baudrillard, Jean. 1998. *The Consumer Society: Myths and Structures*. Thousand Oaks: Sage.

Bauman, Zygmunt. 1997. *Postmodernity and its Discontents*. Cambridge: Polity.

Bayley, David. H., and Clifford Shearing. 1996. "The future of policing." *Law and Society Review* 30(3): 585–606.

Beck, Ulrich. 1992. *Risk Society: Towards a New Modernity*. London: Sage.

Beck, Ulrich. 1999. *World Risk Society*. Malden: Polity Press.

Becker, James F. 1977. *Marxian Political Economy: An Outline.* Cambridge: Cambridge University Press.

Bentham, Jeremy. 1822. "Analysis of the influence of natural religion on the temporal happiness of mankind." Pp. 421–50 in *Jeremy Bentham's Economic Writings*, ed. Werner Stark. London: George Allen and Unwin.

Bentham, Jeremy. 1838. "The Hard-Labour Bill." Pp. 1–35, Part IV in *The Works of Jeremy Bentham*, 11 vols., ed. John Bowring. Edinburgh: William Tait.

Bentham, Jeremy. 1995 [1787]. *The Panopticon Writings*, ed. Miran Bozovic. London: Verson.

Black, Edwin. 2001. *IBM and the Holocaust: The Strategic Alliance between Nazi Germany and America's Most Powerful Corporation*, 1st edn. New York: Crown Publishers.

Bogard, William. 1996. *The Simulation of Surveillance: Hypercontrol in Telematic Societies.* Cambridge: Cambridge University Press.

Boghosian, Heidi. *Spying on Democracy: Government Surveillance, Corporate Power, and Public Resistance.* New York: City Lights.

Braudel, Fernand. 1973. *Capitalism and Material Life 1400–1800*, trans George Weidenfeld and Nicolson Ltd. New York: Harper and Row.

Braverman, Harry. 1975. *Labor and Monopoly Capital; The Degradation of Work in the Twentieth Century.* New York: Monthly Review Press.

Broad, Dave. 2000. *Hollow Work, Hollow Society: Globalization and the Casual Labour Problem in Canada.* Halifax: Fernwood.

Brown, Lorne, and Caroline Brown. 1978. *An Unauthorized History of the RCMP (2ed.).* Toronto: Lewis and Samuel.

Button, Mark. 2007. *Security Officers and Policing: Powers, Culture and Control in the Governance of Private Space.* Aldershot: Ashgate.

Carchedi, Guglielmo. 1977. *On the Economic Identification of Social Classes.* London: Routledge & Kegan Paul.

Carson, Kevin A. 2007. *Studies in Mutualist Political Economy.* Charleston: Booksurge, <http://www.booksurge.com>.

Castel, Robert. 1991. "From 'dangerousness' to risk." Pp. 281–98 in *The Foucault Effect: Studies in Governmentality*, eds Graham Burchell, Colin Gordon, and Peter Miller. Chicago: University of Chicago Press.

Chadwick, Edwin. 1842. *The Sanitary Conditions of the Labouring Population.* London: printed by W. Clowes and sons for H. M. Stationery Office.

Chomsky, Noam. 1994. *World Orders, Old and New.* New York: Columbia University Press.

Chomsky, Noam. 2012. *Occupy.* London and New York: Penguin.

Christie, N. 1993. *Crime Control as Industry*. London: Routledge.

Christie, Nils. 1986. "Suitable enemies." Pp. 42–54 in *Abolitionism: Toward a Non-Repressive Approach to Crime*, eds H. Bianchi, and R. Van Swaaningen. Amsterdam: Free University Press.

Cockerell, H. A. L. and Edwin Green. 1976. *The British Insurance Business, 1547–1970*. London: Heinemann Educational.

Colquhoun, Patrick. 1800a. *A Treatise on the Commerce and Police of the River Thames*. London: Joseph Mawman.

Colquhoun, Patrick. 1800b [1795]. *Treatise on the Police of the Metropolis, etc.* London: Mawman.

Colquhoun, Patrick. 1806. *Treatise on Indigence*. London: J. Hatchard.

Colquhoun, Patrick. 1814. *A Treatise on the Wealth, Power, and Resources of the British Empire*. London: Joseph Mawman.

Cueno, Carl J. 1982. "Class struggle and the measurement of the rate of surplus value." *Canadian Review of Sociology and Anthropology* 19(3): 377–425.

Cunningham, W. C., J. J. Strauchs, and C. W. Van Meter. 1990. *Private Security Trends 1970–2000: The Hallcrest II*. MacLean: Hallcrest Systems Inc.

Currie, Elliot. 1997. "Market, crime and community: Toward a mid-range theory of post-industrial violence." *Theoretical Criminology: An International Journal* 1(2): 147–72.

Dafnos, Tia. 2013. "Pacification and indigenous struggles in Canada." *Socialist Studies/Études socialistes* 9(2): 57–77.

Dawson, Andy. 2014. "Robot security guard is a cross between R2-D2 and Wall-E's girlfriend." in *Mirror.com*. London: Daily Mirror, <http://www.mirror.co.uk/news/technology-science/technology/robot-security-guard-cross-between-4622495> (accessed October 2015).

Day, Richard J. F. 2005. *Gramsci is Dead: Anarchist Currents in the Newest Social Movements*. Toronto: Between the Lines.

de Waard, Jaap. 1999. "The private security industry in international perspective." *European Journal on Criminal Policy and Research* 7: 143–74.

Douglas, Mary, and Baron Isherwood. 1996. *The World of Goods: Towards an Anthropology of Consumption*. New York: Routledge.

Doyle, Aaron, and Richard Ericson. 2004. *Uncertain Business: Risk, Insurance and the Limits of Knowledge*. Toronto: University of Toronto Press.

Eick, Volker. 2006. "Preventive urban discipline: Rent-a-cops and neoliberal glocalization in Germany." *Social Justice* 33(3): 1–19.

Eick, Volker, and Kendra Briken (eds). 2014. *Urban (In)security: Policing the Neoliberal Crisis*. Ottawa: Red Quill Books.

Emsley, Clive. 1991. *The English Police: A Political and Social history*, 2ed. New York: Harvester Wheatsheaf and St. Martin's Press.

Emsley, Clive. 1999a. *Gendarmes and the State in Nineteenth-Century Europe*. Oxford: Oxford University Press.

Emsley, Clive. 1999b. "A typology of nineteenth century police." *Deviance et Societe* 3(1): 29–44.

Ericson, Richard V. 2007. *Crime in an Insecure World*. Cambridge: Polity Press.

Ericson, Richard V., and Kevin D. Haggerty. 1997. *Policing the Risk Society*. Toronto: University of Toronto Press.

Ericson, Richard V., Kevin D. Haggerty, and Kevin D. Carriere. 1993. "Community policing as communications policing." Pp. 37–70 in *Community Policing: Comparative Aspects of Community Oriented Police Work*, eds Dieter Dölling, and Thomas Feltes. Holzkirchen: Felix-Verlag.

Everitt, Alan. 1967. "Farm labourers." Pp. 396–465 in *The Agrarian History of England and Wales*, 8 vols., ed. Joan Thirsk. Cambridge: Cambridge University Press.

Ewald, Francois. 1991. "Insurance and risk." Pp. 197–210 in *The Foucault Effect: Studies in Governmentality*, eds Graham Burchell, Colin Gordon, and Peter Miller. Chicago: University of Chicago Press.

Ewick, Patricia. 1993. "Corporate cures: The commodification of social control." *Studies in Law, Politics, and Society* 13: 137–57.

Fanon, Frantz. 1963. *The Wretched of the Earth*. New York: Grove P.

Fernandez, Luis. 2008. *Policing Dissent: Social Control and the Anti-globalization Movement*. New Brunswick: Rutgers University Press.

Fernandez, Luis, and Christian Scholl. 2014. "The criminalization of global protest: The application of counter-insurgency." Pp. 275–98 in *Urban (In)security: Policing the Neoliberal Crisis*, eds Volker Eick, and Kendra Briken. Ottawa: Red Quill Books.

Fielding, Sir John. 1775. *A Plan for Preventing Robberies within 20 Miles of London*. London: A. Millar.

Fiona Ehlers, Julia Amalia Heyer, Horand Knaup, Peter Müller, Ralf Neukirch, René Pfister, Christoph Schult and Timo Steppat. 2015. "A government divided: Schäuble's push for Grexit puts Merkel on defensive." *Speigel Online*, July 17, 2015: <http://www.spiegel.de/international/germany/schaeuble-pushed-for-a-grexit-and-backed-merkel-into-a-corner-a-1044259.html> (accessed October 2015).

Foucault, Michel. 1973. *The Birth of the Clinic*. London: Tavistock.

Foucault, Michel. 1977. *Discipline and Punish*, trans. A. Sheridan. New York: Vintage Books.

Foucault, Michel. 1980. *Power/Knowledge: Selected Interviews and Other Writings*, ed. Colin Gordon. New York: Pantheon Books.

Foucault, Michel. 1991. "Governmentality." Pp. 87–104 in *The Foucault Effect: Studies in Governmentality*, eds Graham Burchell, Colin Gordon, and Peter Miller. Chicago: University of Chicago Press.

Foucault, Michel. 2003. *"Society Must be Defended": Lectures at the Collège de France, 1975–1976*, trans. David Macey. New York: Picador.

Franklin, James. 2001. *The Science of Conjecture: Evidence and Probability before Pascal*. Baltimore: Johns Hopkins University Press.

Furedi, Frank. 1997. *Culture of Fear: Risk Taking and the Morality of Low Expectation*. Harrison: Continuum Publications.

Gandy, Oscar H. 1993. *The Panoptic Sort: A Political Economy of Personal Information*. Boulder: Westview Press.

Garland, David. 2003. "The rise of risk." Pp. 48–86 in *Risk and Morality*, eds Richard V. Ericson, and Aaron Doyle. Toronto: University of Toronto Press.

Giddens, Anthony. 1991. *Modernity and Self-Identity: Self and Society in the Late Modern Age*. Cambridge: Polity Press.

Gilmore, Joanna, J. M. Moore, and David Scott (eds). 2013. *Critique and Dissent: An Anthology to Mark 40 Years of the European Group for the Study of Deviance and Social Control*. Ottawa: Red Quill Books.

Gough, Ian. 1972. "Marx's theory of productive and unproductive labor." *New Left Review* 76 (Nov–Dec): 47–72.

Graeber, David. 2008. *Direct Action: An Ethnography*. Oakland: AK Press.

Graeber, David. 2009. *Direct Action: An Ethnography*. Oakland: AK Press.

Graham, Stephen. 2010. *Cities under Siege: The New Military Urbanism*. London and New York: Verso.

Gramsci, Antonio. 1971. *Selections from Prison Notebooks*. London: New Left Books.

Greengrass, Mark. 1996. "English projectors and contingency planning in the later seventeenth century." Herzog August Bibliothek, Wolfenbüttel: Paper presented at Publicists and Projectors in Seventeenth-Century Europe Conference.

Greenwald, Glenn. 2014. *No Place to Hide: Edward Snowden, the*

N.S.A., and the U.S. Surveillance State. New York: Metropolitan Books.

Guevara, Ernesto. 1961. *Guerrilla Warfare*. Harmondsworth: Penguin.

Hacking, Ian. 1975. *The Emergence of Probability*. Cambridge: Cambridge University Press.

Hacking, Ian. 1990. *The Taming of Chance*, Ideas in Context. Cambridge and New York: Cambridge University Press.

Hadden, Richard W. 1994. *On the Shoulders of Merchants: Exchange and the Mathematical Conception of Nature in Early Modern Europe*, Suny Series in Science, Technology, and Society. Albany: State University of New York Press.

Haggerty, Kevin. 2003. "From risks to precaution: The rationalities of personal crime convention." Pp. 193–214 in *Risk and Morality*, eds Richard Ericson, and Aaron Doyle. Toronto: University of Toronto Press.

Hall, Steve, and Simon Winlow. 2015. *Revitalizing Criminological Theory: Towards a New Ultra-realism*. Abingdon: Routledge.

Hall, Steve, Simon Winlow, and Craig Ancrum. 2008. *Criminal Identities and Consumer Culture*. Collumpton: Willan.

Halper, Jeff. 2015. *War against the People: Israel, the Palestinians and Global Pacification*. London: Pluto Press.

Hammond, J. L., and Barbara Hammond. 1920. *The Village Labourer: 1760–1832*. London: Longmans, Green and Co.

Hardt, Michael, and Antonio Negri. 2001. *Empire*. Cambridge, MA: Harvard University Press.

Harvey, David. 2004. "The new imperialism: Accumulation by dispossession." Pp. 64–87 in *Socialist Register 2004*, eds Leo Panitch, and Colin Leys. Toronto: Fernwood.

Harvey, David. 2013. *Rebel Cities: From the Right to the City to the Urban Revolution*. London: Verso.

Heath, Joseph, and Andrew Potter. 2005. *The Rebel Sell: Why the Culture Can't Be Jammed*. Toronto: HarperPerrenial.

Henry, Aaron. 2013. "The perpetual object of regulation: Privacy as pacification." *Socialist Studies/Études socialistes* 9(2): 94–110.

Herman, Edward S., and Noam Chomsky. 1988. *Manufacturing Consent: The Political Economy of the Mass Media*. New York: Pantheon Books.

Heroux, Gaetan. 2011. "War on the poor: Urban poverty, target policing and social control." Pp. 107–34 in *Anti-Security*, eds Mark Neocleous, and George S. Rigakos. Ottawa: Red Quill Books.

Hewitt, Steve. 2002. *Spying 101: The RCMP's Secret Activities at*

Canadian Universities, 1917–1997. Toronto and Buffalo: University of Toronto Press.

Houston, David. 1997. "Productive and unproductive labor: Rest in peace." *Review of Radical Political Economics* 29(1): 131–47.

Hoyt, L. 2005. "The business improvement district: An internationally diffused approach to revitalization." Washington, D.C.: International Downtown Association.

Hunt, Alan. 2003. "Risk and everyday life." Pp. 165–92 in *Risk and Morality*, eds Richard Ericson, and Aaron Doyle. Toronto: University of Toronto Press.

Hunt, E. K. 1979. "The categories of productive and unproductive labor in Marxist economic theory." *Science and Society* 43(3): 303–25.

Hunt, Linda. 1991. *Secret Agenda: The United States Government, Nazi Scientists, and Project Paperclip, 1945 to 1990*, 1st edn. New York: St. Martin's Press.

Hyman, Richard. 1971. *Marxism and Sociology of Trade-Unionism*. London: Pluto Press.

Hyman, Richard. 2002. "The future of unions." *Just Labour* 1: 7–15.

Jhally, Sut. 1990 [1987]. *The Codes of Advertising: Fetishism and the Political Economy of Meaning in the Consumer Society*. New York: Routledge.

Johnston, Les. 1992. *The Rebirth of Private Policing*. London: Routledge.

Jones, Trevor, and Tim Newburn. 1998. *Private Security and Public Policing*. New York: Oxford University Press/Clarendon.

Kakalik, J., and S. Wildhorn. 1971. "Private police in the United States." Washington, DC: Government Printing Office.

Kautsky, Karl. 1988. *The Agrarian Question*, 2 vols. London and Winchester, MA: Zwan Publications.

Kellogg, Paul. 1987. "Goodbye to the working class?" *IS* 36(2): 108–10.

Kempa, Michael. 2011. "Public policing, private security, pacifying populations." Pp. 85–106 in *Anti-Security*, eds Mark Neocleous, and George S. Rigakos. Ottawa: Red Quill Books.

Kemshall, Hazel. 2003. *Understanding Risk in Criminal Justice*. Berkshire: Open University Press.

Keynes, John Maynard. 1936. *The General Theory of Employment, Interest and Money*. Cambridge: Cambridge University Press.

KHOU staff news. 2015. "Craigs List ad for Air Jordans leads to arrest over stolen car," April 7, <http://www.khou.com/story/news/crime/2015/04/07/craigslist-ad-for-air-jordans-leads-to-shooting-arrest-over-stolen-car/25398633> (accessed November 2015).

Klein, Naomi. 2000. *No Logo: Taking Aim at the Brand Bullies*. Toronto: Vintage Canada.

Knabb, Ken. 1981. *Situationist International Anthology*. Berkeley: Bureau of Public Secrets.

Kraska, Peter B. (ed.). 2001. *Militarising the American Criminal Justice System: The Changing Roles of the Armed Forces and the Police*. Boston: Northeastern University Press.

Kushnirsky, Fyodor I., and William J. Stull. 1989. "Productive and unproductive labour: Smith, Marx, and the Soviets." Pp. 82–103 in *Perspectives on the History of Economic Thought*, ed. Donald A. Walker, Selected Papers from the History of Economics Society Conference 1987. Aldershot: Gower.

Laclau, Ernesto, and Chantal Mouffe. 1985. *Hegemony and Socialist Strategy: Towards a Radical Democratic Politics*, trans Winston Moore and Paul Cammack. London: Verso.

Lamb, Nicholas, and George Rigakos. 2015. "Pacification through 'intelligence' during the Toronto G20." Pp. 213–39 in *Putting the State on Trial: The Policing of Protest during the G20 Summit*, eds Margaret E. Beare, Nathalie Des Rosiers, and Abigail C. Deshman. Vancouver: UBC Press.

Leadbeater, David. 1985. "The consistency of Marx's categories of productive and unproductive labour." *History of Political Economy* 17(4): 591–618.

Lebowitz, Michael. 2012. *The Contradictions of "Real Socialism": The Conductor and the Conducted*. New York: Monthly Review Press.

Lenin, Vladimir I. 1961. "What is to be done? Burning questions of our movement." Pp. 347–530 in *Lenin Collected Works*. Moscow: Foreign Languages Publishing Press.

Lenin, Vladimir I. 1974. "Reformism in the social democratic movement." Trans. Dora Cox. Pp. 229–41 in *Lenin Collected Works*, vol. 17. Moscow: Progress Publishers.

Lenin, Vladimir I. 1975 [1952]. *Imperialism, the Highest Stage of Capitalism*. Peking: Foreign Languages Press.

Lewis, Michael. 2003. *Moneyball: The Art of Winning an Unfair Game*, 1st edn. New York: W. W. Norton.

Lewis, Michael. 2014. *Flash Boys: A Wall Street Revolt*, 1st edn. New York: W. W. Norton and Company.

Los, Maria. 1995. "Lustration and truth claims: Unfinished revolutions in Central Europe." *Law and Social Inquiry* 20: 117.

Los, Maria, and Andrew Zybertowicz. 2000. *Privatizing the Police State: The Case of Poland*. New York: St. Martin's Press.

Luxemburg, Rosa. 1951. *The Accumulation of Capital*. London: Paul.

Luxemburg, Rosa. 1971. "Women's suffrage and class struggle." Pp. 219–20 in *Selected Political Writings of Rosa Luxemburg*, ed. Dick Howard. New York: Monthly Review Press.

Lynch, Michael J., W. Byron Groves, and Alan Lizotte. 1994. "The rate of surplus value and crime. A theoretical and empirical examination of Marxian economic theory and criminology." *Crime, Law and Social Change* 21(1): 15–48.

Lyon, David. 1994. *The Electronic Eye: The Rise of Surveillance Society*. Minneapolis: University of Minnesota Press.

McGinn, Dave. 2015. "Another study says that too much running is bad for you, but there's more to the story," *Globe and Mail*, February 4, <http://www.theglobeandmail.com/life/health-and-fitness/fitness/why-again-study-that-says-too-much-running-is-bad-is-too-good-to-be-true/article22782320>

MacKinnon, Catharine A. 1982. "Marxism, method, and the state: An agenda for theory." *Feminist Theory* spring: 515–44.

Macpherson, C. B. 1977. *The Life and Times of Liberal Democracy*. Oxford: Oxford University Press.

McMullan, John L. 1996. "The new improved monied police: Reform, crime control, and the commodification of policing in London." *British Journal of Criminology* 36(1): 85–108.

McMullan, John L. 1998. "Social surveillance and the rise of the 'police machine'." *Theoretical Criminology* 2(1): 93–117.

Mandel, Ernest. 1975. *Late Capitalsim*. London: NLB.

Mandel, Ernest. 1976 [1867]. "Introduction to Capital Vol.1." Trans. Ben Fowkes. Pp. 11–86 in Marx, Karl. *Capital, I*. New York: Penguin.

Mandel, Ernest. 1995 [1980]. *Long Waves of Capitalist Development: A Marxist Interpretation*. London: Verso.

Manolov, Martin. 2012. "Anti-security: Q and A interview of George S. Rigakos." *Annual Review of Interdisciplinary Justice Research* 12: 9–26.

Marx, Karl. 1842. "Debates on the law of thefts of wood." *Rheinische Zeitung* 298 (Supplement 1 and 2): 18–32.

Marx, Karl. 1904. *A Contribution to the Critique of Political Economy* Chicago: C.H. Kerr.

Marx, Karl. 1972a. *Theories of Surplus-Value, I*, trans. Jack Cohen. London: Lawrence and Wishart.—. 1972b. *Theories of Surplus-Value, III*, trans. Jack Cohen. London: Lawrence and Wishart.

Marx, Karl. 1973. *Grundrisse*, trans. Martin Nicolaus. New York: Penguin.

Marx, Karl. 1976a [1867]. *Capital, I*, trans. Ben Fowkes. New York: Penguin.

Marx, Karl. 1976b [1867]. *Capital, III*. New York: Penguin.

Marx, Karl. 1978a. *Capital, II*, trans. David Fernbach. New York: Penguin.

Marx, Karl. 1978b. "On the Jewish question." Pp. 26–52 in *The Marx-Engels Reader, 2d.*, ed. Robert C. Tucker. New York: W. W. Norton and Company.

Marx, Karl. 1997. "Capital, Volume II." P. 134 in *Karl Marx and Frederik Engels Collected Works*, Vol. 32, ed. Frederik Engels. Moscow: Progress Publishers.

Mayer, Gerald. 2004. "Union membership trends in the United States." Washington, D.C.: Congressional Report Series.

Midler, Paul. 2009. *Poorly Made in China: An Insider's Account of the Tactics behind China's Production Game*. Hoboken: Wiley.

Miles, Angela R. 1983. "Economism and feminism: Hidden in the household. A comment on the domestic labour debate." *Studies in Political Economy* 11: 197–209.

Miliband, Ralph. 1970. "The capitalist state: Reply to N. Poulantzas." *New Left Review* Jan–Feb: 53–60.

Miliband, Ralph. 1973. "Poulantzas and the capitalist state." *New Left Review* Nov–Dec: 83–92.

Mills, Richard Charles. 1974. *The Colonization of Australia (1829–42): The Wakefield Experiment in Empire Building*. Sydney: Sydney University Press.

Mirchandani, Kiran, and Wendy Chan. 2007. *Criminalizing Race, Criminalizing Poverty: Welfare Fraud Enforcement in Canada*. Black Point: Fernwood Pub.

Mohun, Simon. 1996. "Productive and unproductive labor in the Labor Theory of Value." *Review of Radical Political Economics* 28(4): 30–54.

Mythen, Gabe. 2004. *Ulrich Beck: A Critical Introduction to the Risk Society*. London: Pluto Press.

Nash, Gary B. 1970. *Class and Society in Early America*. Englewood Cliffs: Prentice-Hall.

Neocleous, Mark. 2000. *The Fabrication of Social Order: A Critical Theory of Police Power*. London: Pluto Press.

Neocleous, Mark. 2007. "Security, commodity, fetishism." 35(3): 339–55.

Neocleous, Mark. 2008. *Critique of Security*. Edinburgh: Edinburgh University Press.

Neocleous, Mark. 2010. "War as peace, peace as pacification." *Radical Philosophy* 159: 8–17.

Neocleous, Mark. 2013a. "Air power as police power." *Environment and Planning D: Society and Space* 31: 578–93.

Neocleous, Mark. 2013b. "The dream of pacification: Accumulation, class war, and the hunt." *Socialist Studies/Études socialistes* 9(2): 7–31.

Neocleous, Mark. 2013c. "Unmanning the manhunt: Vertical security, class war, and the hunt." *Socialist Studies/Études socialistes* 9(2): 7–31.

Neocleous, Mark. 2014. *War Power, Police Power*. Edinburgh: Edinburgh University Press.

Neocleous, Mark, and George S. Rigakos 2011. "Anti-security: A declaration." Pp. 15–21 in *Anti-Security*. Ottawa: Red Quill Books.

Nicholson, Linda. 1985. "Feminism and Marx: Integrating kinship with the economic." *PRAXIS International*: 367–80.

Noble, David F. 1986. *Forces of Production: A Social History of Industrial Automation*. New York: Oxford University Press.

Nock, Albert Jay. 1972. *Our Enemy, the State*. New York: Arno.

O'Malley, Pat. 1991. "Legal networks and domestic security." *Studies in Law, Politics, and Society* 11: 171–90.

O'Malley, Pat. 2001. "Discontinuity, government and risk: A response to Rigakos and Hadden." *Theoretical Criminology* 5(1): 85–92.

Ozcan, Gulden, and George S. Rigakos. 2014. "Pacification." in *The Wiley Blackwell Encyclopedia of Globalization*, ed. George Ritzer. Hoboken: Wiley.

Panitch, Leo, and Sam Gindin. 2012. *The Making of Global Capitalism: The Political Economy of American Empire*. London and New York: Verso.

Papanicolaou, Georgios, and George S. Rigakos. 2014. "Democratizing the police in Europe with a particular emphasis on Greece." Athens: Nicos Poulantzas Institute and Transform! European Network.

Papanicolaou, Georgios, and George S. Rigakos. 2015. "Golden Dawn and the 'Dark Forces'," *Jacobin Magazine*, February 24, 2015, <https://http://www.jacobinmag.com/2015/02/greece-syriza-police-reform> (accessed October 2015).

Parenti, Christian. 2003. *The Soft Cage. Surveillance in America: From Slave Passes to the War on Terror*. New York: Basic Books.

Paul, Daniel N. 1993. *We Were Not the Savages: A Micmac Perspective on the Collision of European and Aboriginal Civilizations*. Halifax: Nimbus.

Perelman, Michael. 1983. *Classical Political Economy: Primitive Accumulation and the Social Division of Labor*. Totowa: Rowan and Allenheld.

Perelman, Michael. 2000. *The Invention of Capitalism: Classic Political Economy and the Secret History of Primitive Accumulation*. Durham, NC: Duke University Press.

Perelman, Michael. 2001. "The secret history of primitive accumulation and classical political economy." *The Commoner* 2: 1–21, <http://www.commoner.org>.

Petty, Sir William. 1927a [c. 1690]. *The Petty Papers: Some Unpublished Writings (Vol. 1)*, ed. Marquis of Lansdowne, London: Constable.

Petty, Sir William. 1927b [circa 1690]. *The Petty Papers: Some Unpublished Writings (Vol. 2)*, ed. Marquis of Lansdowne. London: Constable.Piketty, Thomas. 2014. *Capital in the Twenty-First Century*. Cambridge, MA: Belknap Press.

Ponting, Samantha, and George S. Rigakos. 2014. "'To take an accompt of all persons and things going in and out of the citty': Walls as techniques of pacification." Pp. 58–106 in *Urban (In)security: Policing the Neoliberal Crisis*, eds Volker Eick, and Kendra Briken. Ottawa: Red Quill Books.

Postman, Neil. 1985. *Amusing Ourselves to Death: Public Discourse in the Age of Show Business*. New York: Viking.

Poulantzas, Nicos. 1969. "The problem of the capitalist state." *New Left Review* Nov–Dec: 63–78.

Poulantzas, Nicos. 1976. "The capitalist state: A reply to Miliband and Laclau." *New Left Review* Jan–Feb: 63–83.

Poulantzas, Nicos. 2014 [1980]. *State, Power, Socialism*, trans. Patrick Camiller. London: Verso.Priest, George L. 1990. "The new legal structure of risk control." *Daedalus* 119: 207–27.

Proudhon, P. J. 1966 [1840]. *What is Property? An Enquiry into the Principle of Right and of Government*. New York: H. Fertig.

Quan, Douglas. 2012. "Despite the Bad Press, the RCMP Brand Is Still 'Strong'." *Ottawa Citizen*. <http://www.ottawacitizen.com/entertainment/Despite+press+RCMP+brand+still+strong/6864084/story.html> (accessed October 2015).

Reiman, Jefferey. 1995. *The Rich Get Richer and the Poor Get Prison*, 4th edn. Needham Heights: Allyn and Bacon.

Rigakos, George S. 1999. "Hyperpanoptics as commodity: The case of the parapolice." *Canadian Journal of Sociology* 23(1): 381–409.

Rigakos, George S. 2000. "The significance of economic trends for the future of police and security." Pp. 176–9 in *Police and Security:*

What the Future Holds, ed. Jane Richardson. Ottawa: Canadian Association of Chiefs of Police.

Rigakos, George S. 2001. "On continuity, risk and political economy: A response to O'Malley." *Theoretical Criminology* 5(1): 93–100.

Rigakos, George S. 2002. *The New Parapolice: Risk Markets and Commodified Social Control*. Toronto: University of Toronto Press.

Rigakos, George S. 2005. "Beyond public–private: Toward a new typology of policing." Pp. 260–319 in *Re-Imagining Policing in Canada*, ed. Dennis Cooley. Toronto: University of Toronto Press.

Rigakos, George S. 2008. *Nightclub: Bouncers, Risk and the Spectacle of Consumption*. Montreal: McGill-Queen's University Press.

Rigakos, George S. 2011. "'To extend the scope of productive labour': Pacification as a Police Project." Pp. 57–83 in *Anti-Security*, eds George Rigakos, and Mark Neocleous. Ottawa: Red Quill Books.

Rigakos, George S. 2012. "The Downtown Yonge BIA Safety and Security Tracking Study." Toronto: Downtown Yonge Business Improvement Association.

Rigakos, George S. 2014. "Business Improvement as Urban Pacification." Paper presented at the Critical Legal Studies conference, University of Sussex, Brighton, U.K., 5 September.

Rigakos, George S., and Aysegul Ergul. 2011. "Policing the industrial reserve army: An international study." *Crime, Law and Social Change* 56(4): 329–71.

Rigakos, George S., and Aysegul Ergul. 2013. "The pacification of the American working class: A longitudinal study." *Socialist Studies* 9(2): 167–98.

Rigakos, George S., and Richard W. Hadden. 2001. "Crime, capitalism and the risk society: Towards the same olde modernity?" *Theoretical Criminology* 5(1): 61–84.

Rigakos, George S., and Georgios Papanicolau. 2003. "The political economy of Greek policing: Between neo-liberalism and the sovereign state." *Policing and Society* 13(3): 271–304.

Rigakos, George S., Francis Kwashie, and Stephen Bosanac. 2005. "The San Romanoway Community Revitalization Project: Interim report." Ottawa: National Crime Prevention Centre.

Rigakos, George S., John L. McMullan, Joshua Johnson, and Gulden Ozcan (eds). 2009. *A General Police System: Political Economy and Security in the Age of Enlightenment*. Ottawa: Red Quill Books.

Rimke, Heidi. 2011. "Security: Resistance." Pp. 191–216 in *Anti-security*, eds Mark Neocleous, and George S. Rigakos. Ottawa: Red Quill Books.

Roper, Carl A. 2014. *Trade Secret Theft, Industrial Espionage, and the China Threat*. Boca Raton: CRC Press.

Rothbard, Murray Newton. 1975. *A New Land, a New People: The American Colonies in the Seventeenth Century*. Conceived in Liberty, Vol. 1. New Rochelle: Arlington House Publishers.

Saborio, Sebastian. 2013. "The pacification of the favelas: Mega-events, global competitiveness, and the neutralization of marginality." *Socialist Studies/Études socialistes* 9(2): 130–45.

Sanders, Trevor. 2003. "Rise of the rent-a-cop." Ottawa: Law Commission of Canada.

Schulte-Bockholt, Alfried. 2004. "A Neo-Marxist explanation of organized crime." *Critical Criminology* 10(3): 225–42.

Seumas Milne. 2015. "Syriza Can't Just Cave In. Europe's Elites Want Regime Change in Greece." *The Guardian*. 1 July. <http://www.theguardian.com/commentisfree/2015/jul/01/syriza-cave-in-elites-regime-change> (accessed October 2015).

Shantz, Jeff. 2014. "On the criminalization of dissent: Deconstructing official oppression in an age of neoliberalism." *ACJS Today* 29(1): 17–27.

Shearing, C. D., and Jennifer Wood. 2006. *Imagining Security*. London: Willan Publishing.

Shearing, Clifford D., and Philip C. Stenning. 1983. "Private security: Implications for social control." *Social Problems* 30(5): 498–505.

Shearing, Clifford D., and Philip C. Stenning. 1987a. "Reframing policing." Pp. 9–18 in *Private Policing*, eds Clifford D. Shearing, and Philip C. Stenning. Newbury Park: Sage.

Shearing, Clifford D., and Philip C. Stenning. 1987b. "SAY 'CHEESE:' The Disney order that is not so Mickey Mouse." Pp. 317–23 in *Private Policing*, eds Clifford D. Shearing, and Philip C. Stenning. Newbury Park: Sage.

Simon, Jonathan. 1987. "The emergence of a risk society: Insurance, law, and the state." *Socialist Review* 95: 61–89.

Simon, Jonathan. 1994. *Poor Discipline*. Chicago: University of Chicago Press.

Skidelsky, Robert J. 2009. *Keynes: The Return of the Master*. New York: Public Affairs.

Smith, Adam. 1937 [1776]. *The Wealth of Nations*. New York: Random House.

Smith, Adrian. 2013a. "Pacifying the 'armies of offshore labour' in Canada." *Socialist Studies/Études socialistes* 9(2): 78–93.

Smith, Adrian. 2013b. "Pacifying the 'armies of offshore labour' in Canada." *Socialist Studies* 9(2): 78–93.

South, Nigel. 1988. *Policing for Profit*. London: Sage.

Spitzer, Stephen. 1987. "Security and control in capitalist societies: The fetishism of security and the secret thereof." Pp. 43–58 in *Transcarceration: Essays in the Sociology of Social Control*, eds John Lowman, Robert J. Menzies, and Ted S. Palys. Aldershot: Gower.

Stigler, George. 1976. "The success and failures of Professor Smith." *Journal of Political Economy* 84(6): 1,199–213.

Swol, Karen. 1999. "Private security and public policing in Canada." Pp. 15–25 in *The Juristat Reader*. Toronto: Thompson Educational Publishing.

Taylor, Frederick Winslow. 1911. *The Principles of Scientific Management*. New York and London: Harper & Brothers.

Thirsk, Joan. 1984. *The Rural Economy of England: Collected Essays*. London: Hambledon Press.

Thompson, E. 1963. *The Making of the English Working Class*. London: Victor Gollancz.

Tolstoy, Leo, Leo Wiener, and Paul Avrich Collection (Library of Congress). 1961. *The Kingdom of God is Within you; or, Christianity Not as a Mystical Teaching but as a New Concept of Life*. New York: Noonday Press.

Uno, Kozo. 1977 [1964]. *Principles of Political Economy: Theory of a Purely Capitalist Society*, trans. Thomas T. Sekine. Sussex: Harvester Press.

van Steden, Ronald. 2007. *Privatizing Policing: Describing and Explaining the Growth of Private Security*. Amsterdam: Boom Juridische uitgevers.

Volkov, Vadim. 2002. *Violent Entrepreneurs: The Use of Force in the Making of Russian Capitalism*. Ithaca: Cornell University Press.

Von Mises, Ludwig. 1996 [1949]. *Human Action: A Treatise on Economics*, 4th rev. edn. Irvington-on-Hudson: Foundation for Economic Education.

Wakefield, Alison. 2003. *Selling Security: The Private Policing of Public Space*. Devon: Willan Publishing.

Wakefield, Edward Gibbon. 1834. *England and America. A Comparison of the Social and Political State of Both Nations*. New York: Harper & Brothers.

Wakefield, Edward Gibbon. 1849. *A View of the Art of Colonization, with Present Reference to the British Empire*. London: J. W. Parker.

Wall, Tyler. 2013. "Unmanning the police manhunt: Vertical security as pacification." *Socialist Studies/Études socialistes* 9(2): 32–56.

Wallerstein, Immanuel Maurice. 1976. *The Modern World-system:*

Capitalist Agriculture and the Origins of the European World-economy in the Sixteenth Century. New York: Academic Press.

Wilensky, H. 1961. "The uneven distribution of leisure: The impact of economic growth on 'free time'." *Social Problems* 9: 35–56.

Wolff, Richard D. 2011. "The Keynesian revival: a Marxian critique." Pp. 103–14 in *Saving Global Capitalism: Interrogating Austerity and Working Class Resoonses to Crises*, eds Carlo Fanelli, Chris Hurl, Priscillia Lefebvre, and Gulden Ozcan. Ottawa: Red Quill Books.

Wolff, Richard D., and David Barsamian. 2012. *Occupy the Economy: Challenging Capitalism*. San Francisco: City Lights Publishers.

Wood, Stephen. 1982. *The Degradation of work?: Skill, Deskilling, and the Labour Process*. London: Hutchinson.

Index